JAIME JORGE

No More Broken Strings

THE JAIME JORGE STORY

Pacific Press® Publishing Association
Nampa, Idaho
Oshawa, Ontario, Canada
www.pacificpress.com

Edited by Susan Harvey
Designed by Michelle C. Petz
Cover photos by John Sinclair

Copyright © 2002 by
Pacific Press® Publishing Association
Printed in the United States of America

Additional copies of this book may be purchased at
http://www.pacificpress.com

ISBN 0-8163-1905-7

05 06 • 5 4 .

This book is dedicated to my dear wife Emily.

Words cannot fully express my love for you. I thank and praise God every day for bringing us together. Your unconditional love and radiant smile make it possible for me to deal with the lonely moments when I'm without you. When you tell me you miss me, I am able to better understand how much more our heavenly Father yearns for us to commune with Him, and to come home to Him. I love you forever.

I am most fortunate to have such a wonderful family. You have taught me love, patience, forgiveness, and so much more:

My beloved parents, Eugenio and Mayda Jorge.
My precious sister, Maydelé Pohl.
Estle and Delores (Mom and Dad) Hall,
Bayba (grandmother Eneida Diaz),
Abuelo (Eugenio Larrea), Leonel, Ronnie and Ashley Hold,
Keith Pohl, (grandma) Gladys Peavey, Janice Peavey.

I'd like to thank the following people for making such a positive impact in my life. My life is enriched because of you:

Steve and Bonnie Peterson, Chuck and Marla Truscott,
Mark and Helena Newmyer,
Walt and Avonne Thompson, Henry and Hilda Niemann, Don
and Alice Merrill,
Herb and Linda Hill, Frank and Evelyn González,
Willard and Eva Bridwell,
Bill and Pat Mutch, Alonzo and Maxine Jones, Robert and
Blanche Ford, Salim Burgos, Stephen Plate, Bill Claytor,
Ilsa Nation, Johne Perlick, Assir DaSilva, Mark Craig,
Paul and Stephen Tucker, Robert Soderblom, Bob Kyte, Ross
Lauterbach, Susan Harvey, Warren Gough, Jerry Thomas.

Contents

CHAPTER ONE

A Cuban Childhood

The airliner dipped below the clouds, and gradually the lights of Havana came into view. My heart pounded. I had waited for this moment since leaving Cuba as a boy of ten, twenty years before. I reached for my wife's hand and we looked into each other's eyes for a brief moment before I turned again to peer through the darkness outside the plane's window. Below me, the city began to take shape, somewhat familiar in memory, and yet alien in reality. Excitement, expectation, fear, and anxiety fought each other for places in my head. I clutched Emily's hand tightly. I was coming home.

For the past seven years, I had been working to get permission to visit my homeland. It had been seven years of waiting and hoping, requests and denials. Finally, through a miraculous series of events, permission was granted, and I was returning as part of a team of pastors and evangelists. I had also invited my close friend, Steve Peterson, to accompany us. For seven hours, we waited in Cancun for a connecting flight to Havana; hours that had seemed like a lifetime. The last leg of the trip from Cancun to Havana had taken only forty-five minutes, but it, too, felt like an eternity. It seemed that all my life I had been waiting for this moment, and now, finally, as our Aero Caribe Airlines plane touched down on the runway of Havana's Jose Martí International airport at 8:00 P.M. on the night of February 13, 2001, the moment was here.

After four more hours of waiting, undergoing interrogation, and having our papers checked and rechecked, Emily and I and my friend Steve were ready to walk out of the Havana terminal, and into a life and a world that I hadn't seen since I was a child. Would I be able to find the people and see the places that were still so vivid, so fresh, in my memory? Would any fragment of that old life still be there?

My memories of growing up in Cuba are a whirling kaleidoscope of colors, smells, tastes, activities, and music, combined with a constant sense of fear and tension. Being a Christian in communist Cuba was difficult, and, even as a little child, I felt it. I can remember being spat upon, laughed at, and singled out for ridicule wherever I went.

My parents did everything they could to shield and protect their children from the harassment and physical threats that they experienced every day. An incident that happened before I was born illustrates the kind of world we lived in. My dad, a young church pastor, was locking up the church late one night. My mother, then about twenty-four years old, and pregnant with me, was with him. A band of young communist thugs surrounded them.

"So you're a Christian!" one of them snarled at my father.

My dad quietly replied, "Yes."

"We've never been in a church, but we understand Christians get baptized," the gangster said, moving closer to my parents. My mother, growing more frightened, moved behind my father.

"How can I help you?" Dad asked.

"Are you planning on baptizing that child your wife is carrying?" the young man asked.

"Yes," Dad said, and the communist stepped forward and spat in his face.

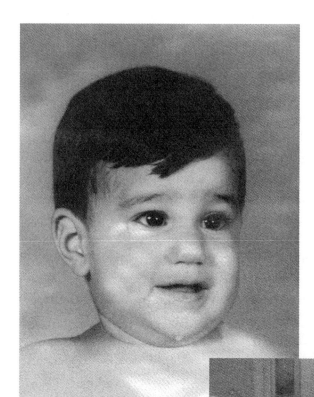

Baby Jaimito

Little Jaime in a special
outfit made by Mima

"Baptize him with that," he sneered, and the gang turned and disappeared into the night.

My family lived their lives quietly, but somehow people always knew we were Christians—probably because we didn't do anything to hide it. My mom tells me that my sister, May, and I used to sing hymns while traveling on the public bus. She hated to tell us to stop, but Christians could go to jail for singing hymns. May, who is three years younger than I am, called our mother "Mima" from the time she could talk. The name stuck. Our mother is still "Mima" to May and me.

Music was always important in our family. Singing and playing instruments are among my earliest memories. I am told that my mother bought me a little plastic eight-key saxophone at age three, and I immediately began learning church tunes.

When I was about five years old, my mother, realizing that I had an affinity for music, asked me a very serious question. "Osito," she said, (Osito was my childhood nickname. In Spanish, it means, "little bear cub.") "what instrument would you like to play?" We decided on the violin. Mima was an accomplished musician herself, playing the violin, the piano, the guitar, the accordion, and, in addition, composing music. She was determined that I would make the most of any talent I had. My parents, at great sacrifice, bought me a tiny quarter-size violin.

And so the lessons began. Twice a week, every week, Mima and May and I rode the bus an hour each way to my violin lessons. The bus was always jam packed with people, and it was nearly impossible to find a seat. Sometimes it was difficult just to get on the bus. My teacher's name was Adolfo Guimbarda, and although I didn't know it at the time, I now realize that he was a great teacher. How fortunate I was to be able to study with him from the very beginning!

I don't remember much about those early lessons. What I do remember is practicing! I had to practice every single day. As far as Mima was concerned, this was not negotiable. At first, I was thrilled with my new violin and enjoyed practicing, but soon the honeymoon was over—and I began what was to become a lifetime habit of trying to get out of my daily practice as often as I could. But Mima stood firm. And she stayed firm, through all of the changes that would come in our lives, for the next fifteen years. When I tired of practicing alone, she would accompany me on the piano. Although she made my early efforts sound so much better, our house was small, and our neighbors were close. I can only imagine the pain I caused those good people with my practicing!

Mima never wavered. "The Lord gave you a talent and you have to use it," she told me. She was equally insistent with my sister, when May was old enough to start piano lessons.

In Cuba, the state forced every child to go to school. We went to school for only four hours every day. Some kids went in the mornings, and some in the afternoons. For some reason, I was always assigned to the afternoons. I'd do my homework in the mornings, and every single day when I came home from school, first I'd practice my violin, and then, if there was any time left, I'd run out to the neighborhood playing field and try to get into a baseball, soccer, or volleyball game.

Growing up in a Cuban *barrio* in the 1970s was tough for a Christian kid. Our neighborhood had once been part of the campus of an Adventist Christian college called El Colegio de Las Antillas, until Castro took it over and changed it into public housing. Because of that, there were several Adventist families living in the neighborhood, and together with other Christians, we were laughed at, mocked, and mistreated.

"We don't play with Christians; get out of here!" the other kids would say. I remember one particularly frightening incident when a bunch of older kids surrounded me after a ball game. The biggest, a foul-mouthed bully named Alexis, poked me in the chest. "You believe in God, don't you?" he asked.

In a squeaky voice, I replied, "Yes."

"There's nothing but a bunch of stupid stories in the Bible," he said. "If there is a God, he's going to have to help you now, because we're going to kill you and cut you up in little pieces. Let's see if your God can put you back together!"

I was sure I was going to die. Even though my parents had taught me to trust in Jesus, I knew these were the same kids I had seen hurting animals and throwing rocks at people. I had even seen them kill a little cat. These were mean kids, and there was no doubt in my mind that they meant to kill me. Before I died, however, I figured I would pray to Jesus and ask Him for help. I closed my eyes. *Jesus, help me,* I prayed. When I opened my eyes, I had lost my fear.

I raised my chin and looked Alexis in the eye. "I'm not afraid of you," I said, my shaky voice growing stronger. "My God is powerful, and if you guys kill me and cut me up, He can put me back together. Anyway, Jesus is coming real soon, and when He returns, I'll be put back together, and I'll live again."

I will never forget the look that came into Alexis's eyes. Like any bully, he had expected to intimidate me into denying my trust in Jesus. He looked down, moved back, and slowly he and the other boys opened up the circle around me. I picked up my bat and ball, and, as they stood and watched with their hands at their sides, I turned for home. As long as I lived there, that group of bullies never bothered me again.

Many times since, I have thought about this experience. Living in the United States now, where we don't have the same anti-Christian pressures, I've tried to remember that kid who stood up for Jesus and was willing to die for Him. If only I had always had that simple, childlike faith!

My mother was largely responsible for instilling a strong faith in me. My pastor father was often away from home, struggling to keep the little band of Christian church members together, but Mima had morning and evening worship with May and me every single day. Today she laughs about my performances at those worships. "Jaimito," she says, "you loved to be the musician, and the preacher, too. First you'd play your violin, then preach a sermon, and then pray, every night. You'd pray for everyone and everything, including the appliances and the furniture." May, too, learned to pray in the same way.

I cherish the memory of the happy hours our family spent in those worship times, learning songs, memorizing Scripture. I have no doubt that that early training made a huge impact on my life. Later, when I became rebellious and turned my back on the Lord and the faithful teachings of my parents, that training helped to bring me back to Jesus. "Train up a child in the way he should go," the Bible says, "and when he is old, he will not depart from it."

The church we attended was an hour away by bus, and each Sabbath our family made that trip. We had no car. The church, like our house, was made of concrete. To me, it seemed very long and narrow, with two rows of pews, and a big pulpit at the front. The building held about 250 people, and I remember that it was always full.

At church, I played my small violin in the orchestra. An amazing number of people played in that orchestra. Later I would learn that in Cuba, Christians couldn't go to college. Many of them studied music instead. We had violinists, wind players, and brass players in the church orchestra, and I looked forward to playing every single weekend.

My sister Maydelé was born when I was three. I loved little May dearly, and spent hours talking to her. I often sneaked into the bedroom to try to pick her up and play with her, while my mother was giving piano lessons or cooking and cleaning. On one occasion, I had been outside in the *barrio,* holding snail races with some of the other kids. I had dirt and snails all over my hands and arms, and for some reason, I chose that moment to try to pick May up to play with her. Mima came in and saw me just as I stood on the top rail of the crib, snails all over me, and May in my arms.

"Jaimito!" she yelled. I got so scared I threw May right back down into her crib and ran away. Luckily, May survived that incident and all the other adventures to which I subjected her.

When I was a child, our house in the *barrio* in the city of Santa Clara seemed big to me, but it was actually quite small—probably no more than 500 square feet. We lived at the end of a row of houses, all connected together. Across the narrow street was an identical row of houses. Like most of the houses in Cuba, all the houses on our street were made of concrete. Inside there was a small living room that also served as both my mother's piano studio and our dining room, and two more little rooms—one where we all slept.

The other room was a little storage/office space where my dad had his big desk. As a boy, I idolized my father, whom I called Pipo (still do). I knew that he had a great passion for the Lord. I loved to go into his little office and sit at his desk when he was gone. I liked to try to open the drawers and look at his papers and all the interesting things he kept there.

Our life was simple. We ate rice and beans just about every day. Plantains (a banana-like fruit) formed a part of our diet. Mima served them many ways, but my favorite was when she cut them in thin slices and fried them like potato chips. We also had lots of avocados. We had an avocado tree in our backyard, and we ate them in every way possible. Pipo loved them so much that he even made avocado milkshakes.

One of my favorite activities as a little boy was to visit my *abuelo* (grandfather), and his wife, Nena. My biological grandmother had died before I was born, and Abuelo had remarried, so Nena had always been my grandmother. Abuelo had a big house—very large by Cuban standards. He had owned the house before the revolution, and had somehow managed to keep it. I remember that I loved to climb and swing on the iron gate at the entrance to his house, pushing myself back and forth until I was swinging rapidly. He also had a swing just outside the front door. May and I loved to sit there and spend hours swinging back and forth.

Abuelo always had special treats and drinks for us. We loved drinking orange soda, which came in bottles much like Coca-Cola. He visited us often, bringing cheese, guava paste, plantains, toys, clothes, and many other gifts. No matter how scarce such things were, he always found a way to get them for us. Whenever he'd see me, he'd give me a big hug and a kiss—and then he'd nibble on my ear—something I absolutely hated. It embarrassed me, but that's not all. I hated that icky, wet earful of saliva! I'd wriggle and squirm and beg him to stop. But Abuelo, bless him, never changed.

As I walked through my old neighborhood on my recent trip to Cuba, I was thrilled to find some of our old neighbors still living there. Emily and I visited with a communist family who had, at one time, been extremely negative and antagonistic toward Christians, and my family in particular. They reminded me of a story that I had completely forgotten. It seems that the communist government had once fined our church a large amount of money. If the church couldn't come up with the cash, the government threatened to close them down. The members gave all they could to help pay the fine, and when that wasn't enough, they began to sell their possessions.

My neighbors told me that they remember seeing me walking through the neighborhood, my arms full of toys. In Cuba, the government allowed each child only three toys a year. Once a year, a shipment of toys and games would come from Russia, and they were rationed, just like everything else. We valued those three toys highly, because they were all we had. I sold my toys to help raise money to keep the church open.

"We were so touched," the neighbors said, "to see you and May and the other Christian kids in the neighborhood, selling your plastic zoo animals and your cars and your dolls to help keep the church open." I wish I could take credit for this unselfish act, but all the credit must go to God, and to my parents, who instilled such principles in their children.

We had little money. Like most Cuban women, my mother stayed home and cared for our family, so we lived on one income—the equivalent of about $50 a month. My mother supplemented my father's meager salary by making plastic flowers, working at this task until late almost every night.

Many people in Cuba made things at home to earn extra money. Mima made her flowers from thick plastic grocery bags, with wire for the stems. Using a pattern, she would cut out the shapes. Then she held the plastic over the gas burner on our stove to soften it and form it into petals. She burned her fingers many times, and often had blisters on them. I remember her saying once that she had singed her eyelashes, bending so close over the open fire.

On certain days, she would go out and sell these flowers. That's how she made the money to pay for a larger violin as I grew, for music lessons, and for the transportation to and from the lessons twice each week. This money also went for extra food and clothing.

In the evenings, sometimes May helped Mima make flowers, while I practiced the violin. Oh, how I hated practicing! Once I acquired a little tape recorder, and came up with a clever scheme. I figured that I could practice for an hour, with the tape recorder running, and then take the next hour off while the tape recorder played. I remember late one night, coming out of my room feeling proud of myself for getting away with this terrific scam, to find my mother and sister toiling away making flowers.

Mima and May looked up from their work as I came into the room, and I felt guilty when I saw my mother's tired face. I felt even worse, however, when May piped up, in her little four-year-old voice. "We're doing this for you," she said, "so you can have money to pay your teacher and learn even more about the violin."

That cut me to the quick and I determined to practice the violin faithfully. And I did—for a while, anyway.

When I was about six years old, I fell ill with rheumatic fever. I don't remember much about this illness, except for feeling tired and weak. I do recall the sad and worried faces of my parents as they took me to the doctor. It seemed that we practically lived in the doctor's office during that year. Miguel Crespo was our family physician. I was impressed with this tall, stately, dignified Christian gentleman. I had noticed that many of the kids in my school were sick much of the time, with runny noses and chronic coughs. At the age of six, I decided that I wanted to be a physician, just like Dr. Crespo, a decision that was to shape my life for many years.

I recovered from rheumatic fever, but the illness left me with a damaged heart. Dr. Crespo gave me a poor prognosis. He told my parents that I would probably not survive beyond my teenage years. They refused to believe this, and, as always, put my life in God's hands. After this illness, I was unusually susceptible to colds and other childhood illnesses.

School was tough for my sister and me. Every morning our teachers expected the entire student body to salute the flag. We lined up by grades, in our school uniforms. Every child was required to wear a red scarf signifying membership in the communist party, but no Christian young person ever wore that scarf. Every morning we lined up with hundreds of other kids, our uniforms complete except for the red scarf. May and I were often singled out, brought to the principal's office, and subjected to questioning. The same questions were put to us repeatedly. "Why aren't you wearing your scarf?" Why are you not a communist?" "You must be a communist—you cannot be a Christian."

So it was amazing that, when I was nine years old, I was chosen to take part in a school competition. My teachers knew that I played the violin, and they selected me to represent the school. I knew that the winner would compete against other schools, and eventually there would be competitions at the provincial level, and even the national level. I passed the first level of competition. The next level took place in an auditorium in my home town of Santa Clara. I had never even been allowed into this auditorium, much less been invited to play there. Ordinarily children were not allowed to go inside. This hall was the home of the Santa Clara Symphony Orchestra. My violin teacher was the concertmaster of this orchestra. I was very nervous. There were participants from dozens of schools. I played a piece called "La Bella Cubana." I knew that I had played my best. Afterwards, some of the judges took me aside.

"We want you to know that you played so well that you deserve to win first place," they said.

My nine-year-old heart swelled. I was so excited to hear that I was going to get a prize. An evil thought crept into my head. *This is a good opportunity to get Mima and Pipo off my back. Now that I've finally accomplished something, maybe they'll ease up on the practicing for a while.*

Then the judges continued, "Now, we understand you're a Christian. You know that we cannot recognize or acknowledge anybody that believes in God in this country. If you are willing to renounce all your beliefs in God, we'll be happy to award you the first place and the prize."

Instantly I remembered my parents telling me that "it is better to obey God, rather than men." I knew what my response to the judges had to be.

Looking up at these tall men with their serious faces, I said, "Thank you very much, but no thank you."

"It's your choice," they shrugged. "It's your loss."

I went home. I was disappointed. I was frustrated and angry as only a nine-year-old can be. My first competition had not ended the way I wanted it to end. Mima and Pipo were disappointed too, but they helped me take comfort from the fact that I had played my best, and had represented my parents, my beloved violin teacher, and my God, to the best of my ability.

Time went by, and a few weeks later, one of the judges came to talk to me once again. He took me alone into a large room. I felt small, sitting in a big chair, at a large, polished table. The judge took a chair across from me. The very air seemed tense, serious. Outside the room, there were government people. I thought they might be soldiers.

"On behalf of the communist government," he said, with something like a smile spreading across his face, "we're prepared to give you the opportunity of a lifetime." He leaned back in his chair. "We would like to give you a scholarship to go to Moscow to study in the best school of music in the world. All you have to do is to renounce all of your religious beliefs."

I said nothing.

"This is a wonderful opportunity for you and your family," he continued. Even at that age, I knew that in Cuba, sports and the arts were the propaganda machines of communism. Great athletes, musicians, and artists are the pride of the government. They and their families had a better lifestyle and more opportunities and privileges than anybody else did.

He leaned forward and rested his folded hands on the table. His face was serious, but not unkind. "I don't care if you believe in God or not. It makes no difference to me. But I have this document here that you must sign." He slid a piece of paper across the table toward me. "This document says that you are renouncing all of your religious beliefs. You don't believe in God anymore. You believe in Lenin, Stalin, Marx, and Castro. That is your belief system. What do you say?"

"Well," I said, "if that's the condition, I guess you already know the answer."

Suddenly his demeanor changed. In a loud, angry voice, he said, "You're wasting my time and the government's time. You're never going to be a good violinist." Abruptly he rose from the table. "You're free to leave," he said.

I was shaken right down to my toes. On wobbly legs, I walked out of the room. For a boy of only nine, this had been a shattering experience. I knew that I was walking away from what seemed to be the opportunity of a lifetime. But my parents had instilled in me that God is in charge—that all things work together for good to those that love God. I thank God for that training, and for the strength He gave me at such a young age to stand up for Him. I walked out of that room with God on my side, and the amazing thing was that God had something so much better in store for me and my family—better than we could ever imagine. Because, not long after that, we were able to leave Cuba.

CHAPTER TWO

Mima and Pipo

Around my eighth birthday, my dad was transferred from the church at Santa Clara to La Esperanza, a little town a few miles away. So my family moved to a much bigger house—with a bedroom for my parents and a separate bedroom for May and me. It had a big patio and a backyard, and even a garage. We were all thrilled to have such a beautiful new house.

Something remarkable happened to me in this house, and I want to tell you about it. The house had two floors, and my parents hardly ever let May or me go upstairs unsupervised, because, at the back of the house, behind my parents' bedroom, was a sort of rooftop porch which had no railing around it. Mima warned us never to open the door that led out onto this porch. Of course, this made it practically irresistible to me.

One Friday afternoon, when Mima was busy working downstairs, I went upstairs, supposedly to take a shower. I decided to open the forbidden door and step out onto the unrailed porch. Some of the neighborhood children were playing behind the house, and I wanted them to see me in this high, unguarded place. Once I had my friends' attention, I began to show off more and more, getting closer to the rooftop edge. Suddenly one of the kids threw something at me—a seedpod or a stone—who knows? I tried to dodge it, and lost my balance. I fell forward, and felt myself falling through the air. For a second, I closed my eyes, and when I opened them again, I was standing upright on the concrete driveway behind the house. I stood there for a split second and looked around, dazed. The two kids who had seen me fall were staring at me, in shock. I was so frightened that I ran back into the house, up the stairs, and into the bathroom.

I remember that I felt a sharp pain in my right leg, and for several months afterwards I had a noticeable limp. When Mima asked why I was limping, I brushed her off. "I'm OK," I said.

Two or three months later, Raisa, a young girl who lived with our family, and who had been one of the kids in the backyard that day, finally told my mother what she had seen. Mima had been questioning her, trying to find out if she knew why I was limping. "I can't keep quiet anymore. I've got to tell you," Raisa confessed. She described to my mother what had happened. I had been standing on the edge of the roof, she told her, and when I fell, I had flipped in the air and landed standing up. I have no doubt that my guardian angel must have helped me do that mid-air flip, or I would have landed on my head. God had intervened, and had prevented my own foolishness from causing me serious harm or even death. Little did I know then that this was to be a pattern that I'd repeat many times. God was going to have to rescue me repeatedly as I continued to go my own headstrong way in life!

School continued to be a struggle. My belief in God caused me to suffer harassment, interrogation, and ridicule. May endured the same thing. We told our parents about these attacks, but there was little they could do.

In spite of these problems in school, I remember that I loved at least one part of it—and that was recess. I considered it my best

My birthday in Cuba at Abuelo's house

Jaime in 1978 in Cuba

My violin teacher,
Adolfo Guimbarda

subject. Despite my frequent illnesses, I had a young boy's usual excess of energy, and whenever recess came, I played and ran around like crazy. However, on many days, my teachers deprived me of recess. Instead, a teacher would talk to me. "You need to be a Young Communist Pioneer. You have to wear your red scarf. We cannot allow you to get away with not wearing your red scarf."

I would reply, "I can't do that."

"Well, you're not going to leave this room until you become a communist."

"I can't do that," I'd repeat. "I love Jesus."

I remember one particular day when missing recess and enduring this lecture meant that I missed a chance to go to the bathroom. I went up to the desk. "Teacher, can I go to the bathroom?" I asked.

"Only if you become a communist," she snapped.

I returned to my seat. The urge got stronger. Several more times I asked her if I could please go to the bathroom. Each time she said No. To my shame, I could not wait any longer to go to the bathroom, and I wet my pants. This caused a great commotion. Somebody had to come and clean it up. The principal came. Finally, my mother came to get me. She was shocked at my pale face, and I told her that I had a splitting headache. She took me home. I felt embarrassed and humiliated by this experience. Yet I remember Mima dealing with me so tenderly, so lovingly. Always she talked to May and me about the love of Jesus, and even though we went through these humiliating experiences on a daily basis, we still loved Jesus. Faithfully, every single day, Mima, and Pipo too, when he could, had worship with us. They gave me a foundation and a love for God. They gave me a trust in Him that I will never abandon.

As May and I got a little older, we began to understand more of the things that were going on in Cuba, and what our parents endured because of their faith in God. Our pastor father was doing his best to minister to both the Christians and the nonbelievers in our community. Often he left just after we woke up in the morning, and he came in late at night—usually after we had gone to bed.

Sometimes he would travel all the way across Cuba to visit prisons where young Christians had been incarcerated for their faith. He spent days on end with them, encouraging them and praying with them.

I missed Pipo, and eagerly looked forward to his coming home from these trips. Often he would bring a special treat for May and me. I remember some delicious little peanut bars called turrrón. We didn't get many of these treats, because everything was rationed. Another special thing he brought home was guava paste with cream cheese—one of my favorite things to eat. Although we didn't get to spend a great deal of time with Pipo, his presence was large in our lives. We knew he was doing God's work, and that he loved us very much.

My father had grown up as the only child in a well-to-do family. His father had managed a large sugar mill, and prior to the revolution and the subsequent communist regime, the family had enjoyed an affluent lifestyle. His mother died of a heart attack when Pipo was a young man. Pipo says he was a rather wild youth, a renegade, who used to walk around the streets with a gun.

In his younger days, Pipo was extremely athletic. Although not an especially tall man, his strong, muscular physique gave the appearance of height. He belonged to a gym, and was a body-builder and a karate expert. At a young age, however, he was also interested in spiritual things. Like most of the Cubans of his day, he was a Roman Catholic. He was studying for the priesthood when he met my mother through a friend. Mima remembers that he had a real flair for the dramatic in his youth. With his black hair and mustache and laughing brown eyes, he swept her off her feet—sometimes arriving for their dates on a black horse, with a rose in his teeth.

Mima was athletic, too. Tall, slender, with lovely light brown hair and brown eyes, she loved sports, especially basketball. She was also musical, and as a little girl, longed to play the piano. Her family was poor, and there was no money for a musical instrument. Mima worked at various jobs, and saved her pennies to buy a piano. Her grandmother, who adored her, helped her earn money, too. This grandmother, whom I was later to know and love as *Abuelita* Nina, kept a pig in their tiny, all-cement backyard. Every day she went around the *barrio* and asked neighbors for leftover food to feed the pig. When the pig became big and fat, she sold it and bought another baby pig. In this way she helped my mother save enough money to buy a piano.

In the meantime, Mima started piano lessons. She made a keyboard from a long piece of cardboard, drawing the keys on with crayons. Every day she practiced on this homemade keyboard, and once a week she went to her teacher's house and played the notes that she had practiced on a real piano. Two years and several pigs later, the family was able to buy her a piano.

Mima has always been studious and hardworking. In fact, she began medical school in Havana, but had to give it up after two years of study. She was asked, as I was later, to renounce God and embrace communism—and was forced to leave medical school when she refused to do so. Fortunately, the government allowed her to return to Santa Clara and study to become a teacher. She's been a teacher ever since. In the United States, she has taught for many years in the public school system.

When Mima and Pipo were dating, a literature evangelist came to the house where Mima lived with her mother. Mima refused to let him in. But Fernando Paulín persisted and returned several times, until Mima relented and allowed him to show her his books. He asked her if he could come back and study the Bible with her.

"Only if I can bring my boyfriend," she replied. Fernando happily agreed to this stipulation, and Mima and Pipo began to take Bible studies together. Both the Bible studies and the time spent together had positive results. My parents were married in April of 1965, and baptized a few months later. Shortly thereafter, Pipo entered the seminary to prepare himself for the ministry.

My parents always taught May and me to trust in Jesus. In the midst of the fear, persecution, and uncertainty of living in communist Cuba, they gave us a secure home life, with Christ as the center. Every night, before we went to bed, they taught us to say this prayer from Psalm 4:8: "I will both lie down in peace and sleep, for you alone, oh Lord, make me dwell in safety."

How can I tell you how important my parents are to me? They are the two greatest people I have ever known. Pipo, with his unswerving dedication to his faith, his uprightness, his determination not to compromise his religion for anything or anybody, has set an example for me that has served as a guiding beacon throughout my life. Mima's courage and devotion to her family and her children, despite all odds, has been equally influential in my life. Mima has suffered from illness all her life. She has a migraine headache almost every day. I don't know how she has been able to accomplish all the things she has. I get migraine headaches, too, once in a while, and when I do, there's nothing I can do except take medication and rest in a darkened room until I feel better. But Mima just keeps going. Her students, her teachers, and her principals have always spoken highly of her skills and her dedication to her work.

When I'm unhappy for some reason, or when I'm facing a tough task, I think about Mima. I think about her blistered fingers from making plastic flowers so that my sister and I could have the things she wanted for us.

CHAPTER THREE

Leaving Cuba

As early as 1960, my father tried to get exit visas for our family to leave Cuba. In 1980, in a last desperate measure, he decided to write a personal letter to Fidel Castro. "I am a Christian minister, Mr. Castro," he wrote. "I have been trying to leave Cuba for the last twenty years because we are not allowed to pursue our religious beliefs here. My family and I are a nuisance and a bother to you, and we go through a great deal of pain and suffering for our faith. I am no good to you. I am not an asset to you, and I would like to ask you if you would be kind enough to allow me and my family to leave this country so that we can practice our faith and our belief in God and worship Him freely."

He sent the letter and a period of anxious waiting followed. Would the letter get to Castro? Would he respond? Would the government single us out for more persecution because of it?

Finally, the response came, but not from Castro. My father was given an appointment to see the head of the department of immigration. This official was known for his cruelty. When Pipo walked into the immigration office, he was asked to take a seat across the desk from the official. Looking down at the desktop, Pipo saw that the man had his letter to Castro in front of him.

"Did you write this letter?" the official asked.

"Yes, I did," Pipo said, sending up a silent prayer and steeling himself for the worst. What was going to happen next?

"We are going to study your case," the official replied. "That will be all. Goodbye." And Pipo was dismissed without learning anything further. He had no idea whether this interview meant we might be allowed to leave—or whether it signified an increase in persecution against us.

Shortly after this strange encounter, we learned that Cuba was allowing some people to go to the United States for the first time since Castro had come to power. Castro was giving permission for Cubans who lived in the United States to come to Cuba by boat and bring their relatives back to America with them.

Pipo got excited again about the possibility of leaving the oppression and persecution of Cuba. We heard that thousands of boats, large and small, were sailing from Florida to Havana's port of Mariel, piloted by Cubans coming to claim their family members. My parents immediately redoubled their efforts to obtain permission for our family to leave. We got in touch with relatives we knew in Florida, and they promised to come get us. As it turned out, it wasn't going to be that simple.

Here is what was happening: People from Florida would submit a list of family members—maybe ten or twelve relatives. The Cuban government would give them clearance to come to Cuba and pick up those people. However, when they arrived, after a long wait for their family members to be processed and allowed to leave, the officials would say, "You can take only two or three of your family—and you have to take these twenty other people with you."

In this way, Castro was emptying out his jails, and under his government's pretense of allowing their families to leave Cuba, he forced Cuban Americans to ferry thousands of criminals to the United States. We learned later that by the time the Mariel Boat Lift was over, Castro had managed to ship 120,000 known criminals to the United States.

Regardless of that, we still hoped and prayed that we could get on one of those boats. For some reason, we were always at the tail end of the processing and our papers never came through. Many months went by. Hope grew and then waned. Opportunities to leave with friends from America came and were lost, because the boats were filled up with criminals and other refugees. Our fears mounted as stories began to filter back to us of hundreds, even thousands of people who lost their lives at sea in little boats that were hopelessly overfilled.

Things at home were tense. We said Goodbye to family members as they found ways to leave the country. Uncle Leonel left. My grandmother, whom we called Bayba, found a way to leave. We watched as family and friends endured acts of repudiation. Some of the communists threatened both those who were leaving and the family members of those who had already left. An angry mob yanked Bayba out of her house, dragged her for an entire block and subjected her to kicks, taunts, and curses. She barely survived with her life. Anger and bitterness ruled the day. Mobs roamed the streets, throwing bottles and rocks at people they suspected of leaving. People who had been given permission to leave were actually killed by mob violence before they could go.

It was a tumultuous time. The government was in turmoil. Castro was determined to rid the country of all criminals and anticommunists. People lied about themselves, hoping the government would deem them undesirable citizens and allow them to leave. "I've been a political prisoner," they'd claim, or "I'm an antirevolutionary." In its haste to rid itself of all undesirables, the government made mistakes, and allowed certain people to slip through.

One such person was Virgilio Monteagudo, a member of our church in Santa Clara. He had been a top communist officer before he gave his heart to the Lord. Former communists were ordinarily never allowed to leave, but miraculously, he and his family were able to get on a boat and leave the country.

Uncle Leonel had a similar experience. He had been an honor student at the University of Havana, and president of the Student Government. He told the government that he was an anticommunist and an antirevolutionary, and somehow managed to get on a boat and come to the United States. In America, he lived with his father, who had left Cuba years before, and enrolled in medical school. Today he is a practicing physician in the United States.

Still our family waited and no word came from the government. The tension increased. It was an especially difficult time for my parents. Mima had aunts, uncles, and cousins who were not attempting to leave at all. Pipo, too, knew he would have to leave family behind, including Abuelo and Nena. Much as my parents wanted to go, leaving family behind was going to be hard.

Then the day came when all of our family members who had been trying to leave Cuba were gone. Only Mima, Pipo, May, and me were left behind. Still we waited. Then Pipo finally got word from the government. They had granted us permission to leave. We never knew whether Pipo's letter had finally reached Castro, or if we were being allowed to leave for some other reason.

On a Saturday night in the fall of 1980, the police cars came to take us to Havana for the final processing. We were excited, but it was also a time of sadness. Many of our neighbors and church friends came to see us off. We were allowed to take almost nothing with us, and we knew that the government would take immediate possession of our house and all its contents, so we gave away all of our belongings, one by one. Towels, dishes, pots, pans, chairs, tables, all went to our friends and neighbors.

The government officials told us we would spend two or three days in Havana, where our final processing would take place before boarding a plane for America. We were interviewed at the American Embassy and given passports and visas. Then we were taken, with thousands of others, to a military base outside Havana called Mosquito Beach. There we were housed in tents to await our imminent departure.

Once again, however, we were disappointed. A storm hit the Gulf of Mexico, which prevented any more boats from coming to Cuba. We waited some more. Then the United States government, realizing that Castro had sent a wave of Cuban criminals to the U.S., put a hold on any further immigration of Cubans. We, along with thousands of others in our tent city, entered into a state of limbo that was to last for more than three months.

It was a horrible time for my parents. They and the other adults in the camp were frightened and worried. Nobody knew what was happening, or whether we would ever be able to leave the country. To make things worse, everyone knew that if we weren't able to get out of Cuba, we had nothing left to go home to.

Conditions in the camp were primitive. We had nothing—only the clothes we were wearing when we left home. There was no privacy—just hundreds and hundreds of canvas cots and bunk beds everywhere you looked.

Food was scarce and very poor. They fed us twice a day. We were given yogurt and pound cake in the morning, and rice and meat in the afternoon. As vegetarians, we often had only rice to eat. Many times we could eat only one meal a day. Often, some or all of the food was rotted or contaminated.

Even with these terrible conditions, for a ten-year-old boy like me, Mosquito Beach was a huge playground. There was an element of fantastic adventure about life in this tent city. There was no school, no organization, and best of all, no violin and no practicing. All day I ran around with other kids in the compound, and we were creative about thinking up things to do. For instance, we loved to climb over the rocks near the ocean and wait for crabs to come out. We snared them with thread and made pets of them.

People did whatever they could to pass the time and keep their spirits up. Some of the men took one of the canvas sleeping cots apart, thread by thread, and rolled the thread into a baseball. Cubans love baseball, and we always had a game going on.

People in the camp made their own card and Monopoly games. They melted down plastic bags and made them into dice and dominoes. Domino tournaments went on late into every night. Mima turned out to be an amazingly good domino player. She and a friend teamed up and beat everybody in the camp. It was great fun for May and me to watch Mima's team beat all the other players.

Pipo's interest in bodybuilding came in handy, too. He started an exercise club in the camp, rigging up weights with rocks, and putting up bars and beams in the trees to do all kinds of exercises.

Our desire to leave Cuba united us all, but with so many people in a confined area with so little to do, some got into trouble, and many fights broke out in the camp. Close friendships were formed, also.

I remember making friends with a young Cuban soldier named Floirán. He was a tall, strong young man, impressive in his olive green uniform and high black leather boots. I loved to hang out with him at the camp headquarters in the center of the compound. Like other kids in the camp, I had been picking up any loose money I found, and during my stay had acquired a handful of change—no more than a dollar or two. When it was time for me to leave, I tried to give my money to Floirán. I'll never forget his sad eyes as he said to me, "I couldn't possibly be allowed to take that money out of this base. I would get into trouble. On your way to the U.S., just throw it into the ocean and say, 'This is for my friend Floirán.' " I didn't comprehend at all, at the time, but now I think Floirán was trying to tell me that he, too, hoped and dreamed of going to America. He just wasn't able to say it outright.

Finally, the day came when trucks and vans began to move in and out of camp, and word got around that we were going to be leaving soon. But more days of waiting, filled with high emotion and confusion, followed. We saw people leaving. We said Goodbye to friends we had made in camp, knowing that we would probably never see them again. At long last, our group was called. We were told that we would all be shuttled by bus to the airport—where we were going to be put on a plane for the United States of America.

Mima had been ill in the camp. She had also broken her foot, which was in a cast, and was hobbling around on crutches. I remember finally boarding our bus in the long line of shuttles, with Pipo helping Mima as she limped slowly up the steps. We were wearing the same clothes that we had worn to leave home in, three months before, now little more than rags. We had very few possessions with us. Pipo had his Bible. Mima had a brown paper bag that contained her most prized possessions—three or four music books that contained all the religious songs and hymns she had written during the years she had been a Christian.

We went through several security checkpoints, and they searched us thoroughly, but allowed Pipo to keep his Bible and Mima her brown paper bag. At the final checkpoint, for some reason, the bag and its contents were confiscated. Mima began to cry inconsolably. We were all so sad for my mother, but Pipo quickly signaled May and me to say nothing. We could do nothing. We knew that if we made a fuss or complained, we might all be left behind. Mima just continued to weep quietly.

As our bus approached the plane, an army captain who had been part of the guard at Mosquito Beach noticed my mother's tears. "Ma'am, what's wrong?" he inquired.

"My life's work, all of my music, all the songs I've written," Mima sobbed. "They were taken away from me."

The captain stopped the whole caravan of shuttle busses, and asked us to wait right where we were. A few minutes later, he came back with Mima's brown paper bag and handed it to her with a slight bow and a smile. Now we knew we had one more thing to be grateful to God for—He had touched that army captain's heart.

We boarded the plane, fastened our seat belts, and began the last short leg of our long journey to freedom. Mima clutched her paper bag in her arms. Forty-five minutes later, we landed in Miami, to begin a new life. We had nothing but our hopes and dreams.

CHAPTER FOUR

A New Life in America

December 3, 1980 is a date I will never forget. On that day we set foot on American soil and experienced freedom for the first time in our lives. What a tremendous feeling it was! We were all in a daze as we were processed and given the necessary permits and identification papers. Then Jesus Azán, Pipo's best friend from elementary school—we called him *El Chino* because of his slanted, laughing eyes—came to pick us up and take us home with him. This dear friend opened up his home to us four ragged Cuban refugees, and we lived with him for nearly a month.

That first day at El Chino's house, I ate grapes and apples for the first time. I had a soft drink. I also did something I had always yearned to do—I chewed some gum. Somebody gave us a huge bag full of the stuff. Nobody told me that you weren't supposed to swallow it. When I learned that you just chew it for a while, then throw it out and chew a new stick, I was amazed.

How can I make you understand what America looked like to a ten-year-old Cuban boy? I was awestruck. The streets were clean and wide. The lights were bright and the colors were vivid. The houses were beautiful. Nothing seemed to be shabby or falling apart. People smiled at me, and treated me courteously. I walked around with my mouth wide open for days.

It was the Christmas season, and I saw Christmas trees and decorations for the first time. We never celebrated Christmas in Cuba. It was not against the law, but was strongly discouraged by the government. Now, Cuban families invited us to Christmas parties. It seemed to me that their homes were palatial, and they had enough food to last a lifetime.

Our friends found kind ways to give us the things we needed, and I soon learned about Santa Claus. The first pair of pants I had in America were a pair of brown corduroys. "Look, Mima," I said, opening the gaily-wrapped package and holding up the garment with the price tag still dangling from it. "Santa Claus only had to spend $10.99 for these pants!"

Pipo found a job at Lindsey's Lumberyard, making $3.35 an hour, and my sister and I started attending public school. We left El Chino's kind hospitality and moved into a little place of our own. Our brothers and sisters in the church generously helped us set up housekeeping, starting us out with a little furniture and some clothing and linens. It soon became apparent, however, that we could not survive on Pipo's $3.35 an hour salary.

We heard from our friend and former church member, Virgilio Monteagudo, whom we had known in Santa Clara. He left Miami shortly after immigrating and moved his family to Milwaukee, Wisconsin. "You ought to move up here," he said. "I'm working for the U.S. government, helping to run a program called UMOS (United Migrant Opportunity Service), that assists families like us. They help with job placement, they teach you English, they help you get your GED. They will help you find a place to live and even pay you a small wage while you study."

Mima and Pipo talked over all the options. Many of our Cuban friends had chosen to stay in Florida. Some of Pipo's fellow pastors were going to Michigan to take English-intensive courses at Andrews University, and from there to job placements in pastorates in the United States. What should they do?

My parents decided on Milwaukee. So in February, we four thin-blooded Cubans boarded an Eastern Airlines jet and flew to Wisconsin and its coldest winter in eighty years. We had almost no winter clothing. A generous church member allowed us to live in a little house she owned, rent-free, while we were getting established. Unfortunately, it had almost no heating. Imagine the four of us, used to hot, humid weather, shivering through that first Wisconsin winter! Snow fell constantly, in fact, a record sixty-nine inches worth, and the temperature didn't get above zero for weeks. Once again, however, we were blessed by the warmth and friendship of our fellow church members. The Milwaukee Spanish church gave us food, clothing, and even financial help when we needed it. Somehow, we managed.

Despite the cold, May and I loved Milwaukee and its snow. Pipo bought us little blue plastic sleds, and we would go to a nearby park, and ride those sleds down what seemed to be a mountain, shouting with glee.

We received our first welfare check in February of 1981, shortly after arriving in Milwaukee. We needed it. We could have purchased food and warm clothing with that money, but I will never forget what my parents did with it instead.

With that check in hand, Mima and Pipo took my sister and me to Milwaukee Junior Academy, and used the money as the down payment on a Christian education for us. In Cuba, we had dreamt of having a Christian education one day. Our parents had brought us to America for this reason. "We didn't come to this country to get worldly wealth or fame," Mima said to me that day. "We came so that you and your sister could have a Christian education, so that you can be prepared to serve the Lord."

School was challenging. I had started the fourth grade in Cuba, and finished it at Milwaukee Junior Academy. I didn't speak any English. There were a few kids in the school from the Spanish church. I quickly became good friends with a kid named Joel Lopez. Joel and I are still friends to this day. He helped me with my English and my schoolwork. Unfortunately, I was much more interested in having a good time than I was in schoolwork. I had discovered straws and spit wads, among other things, and I spent much of my time getting into trouble.

Actually, a lot of the trouble happened simply because I didn't know what the rules were. Not understanding what was being said, I just muddled along the best I could, pretending to know what was going on. This method of dealing with the language problem, combined with my hyperactive behavior and my penchant for mischief, turned out to be a sure-fire recipe for disaster. You would think a kid who was having trouble understanding the language would want to blend in, but not me. I wanted to show off, to stand out from the crowd. Believe me, I did.

Our teacher was a gentleman by the name of Mr. Pelto. He taught grades four, five, and six in one room, sharing his time among the three groups. When he wasn't teaching our fourth grade class, I was busy disrupting it. He kept a little piece of paper under the glass on his desktop. Bad behavior got you a mark on that piece of paper. The rumor was that if you got ten marks, you would get something called *the boot*. I had no idea what *the boot* was. Apparently, nobody had gotten *the boot* during the school year before I came to MJA. I, however, soon became intimately acquainted with it and the school principal, Mr. Beck. Thanks to my bad behavior, that oversized rubber shoe made regular contact with my posterior during the short time I was in that school.

Even though we had little money, our family was happy. We were beginning to absorb the fact that we were living in a free country with infinite possibilities. Pipo bought a used car for $400—an ugly, boxy, olive-green Ford with no heater—but we thought it was

wonderful. After years of living with the rationing of food and clothing, we were thrilled to go to stores and buy whatever we needed—
at least as far as our money would allow. We were still getting food
stamps and public assistance while my parents finished their GED
and English classes. Once a month, we took our car to the grocery
store and filled it up with food. We shopped in Goodwill and other
second-hand stores, and occasionally, we made an exciting trip to
K-mart to buy something new.

Life was beginning to take on a normal everyday feeling. Before
too long, both my parents were working for UMOS, Mima as a
math and English teacher, and Pipo as a counselor and coordinator.
May and I rode the bus to school, and that hour each way was the
most exciting time of the day for me, with all sorts of opportunities
for mischief-making. I spent a lot of time talking to my new friend
Joel and his sister Arleen—my first American crush. The kids at
school treated us kindly for the most part, although some of them
made fun of our old, worn, out-of-style clothes. It struck me funny
sometimes. Now we weren't being taunted for being Christians,
Christians were taunting us for wearing worn-out clothes! America
was a great place!

I had nearly forgotten all about the violin. During the time we
were planning our immigration to America, waiting in the camp,
and getting settled in our new country, I had enjoyed a wonderful
break from practicing. I enjoyed this respite, and saw no reason to
hurry up the process of beginning my music studies again, but my
parents had other ideas. As soon as they learned the right place to
go, they marched me to a building in downtown Milwaukee, where
we climbed several flights of stairs to the offices of an organization
called Music for Youth, sponsored by the Milwaukee Symphony
Orchestra. My vacation from music was over. They had found me a
violin and a teacher.

Music for Youth was a wonderful organization. It existed solely
to encourage and train young musicians. There were actually three
different orchestras involved, with the first one being the most

My first concert with
the Milwaukee Youth
Symphony

One of my first recitals in
the United States (1981)

My baptism with Pastor
Ismael Rojas and his wife
Esther (1981)

advanced. From there, some kids went on to famous music schools, such as Juilliard or Curtiss or Peabody. I auditioned, and at age ten or eleven was assigned as concertmaster of the third and youngest of the orchestras. I spent two years with that orchestra. We practiced every week for three hours, and presented a concert once or twice a season.

That experience was a highlight of my life. I didn't speak much English, so I just played. I didn't even know the names of the notes, because in Cuba, the notes are not assigned letters. I was used to Do Re Mi Fa So La Ti. It was difficult for me to absorb the concept of notes with letter designations, like A B C D E F and G. This language problem caused me a great deal of consternation. Every time the conductor spoke to me, I shook with fear. In pictures from those performances, the fear is obvious on my face.

The school year ended. My grades were pretty bad, although amazingly, somehow I got an A in spelling, even though I still didn't speak much English. My sister, May, just three years younger, learned the language faster than I did, and today she speaks English perfectly without an accent. I still get tongue-twisted sometimes, and I have a sort of Cuban-Midwestern accent that's all my own.

Wisconsin finally warmed up that spring, and my parents sent me to summer camp at Camp Go Seek in the central part of the state. I was excited about going—mainly because I thought it would be great to be away from my family for a whole week. I didn't have a clue what summer camp was. That didn't matter—I was bursting with energy and excitement, and eager to experience it, whatever it was.

I spent that week with a bunch of kids and a counselor named Darwin Elmer in a tent. Everything we did was brand new to me. We had pillow fights every night and I really got into the spirit of them. I didn't realize they were just for fun. One night I put a flashlight inside my pillow, and when some guy hit me, I hit him back, and that flashlight whacked him pretty good. My parents were called in, and there I was, three days after I'd arrived, in the camp director's office, in trouble again. Somehow Mima and Pipo got things straightened out, and I was allowed to stay.

Summer camp was one of the most interesting and challenging things I'd ever done. To begin with, I nearly froze to death. Wisconsin nights, even in summer, can sometimes be cold, especially when you're sleeping in a tent. All the other kids had sleeping bags. I didn't even know what a sleeping bag was. Fortunately, when Mima and Pipo came to bail me out of trouble, they also brought me a sleeping bag.

The biggest challenge, however, was that not one single person on that campground—not a kid, not a grown-up—spoke Spanish, and I still didn't speak English. I had no idea where to go and what to do. Again, I got into trouble because I couldn't understand what was expected of me. That wasn't the only reason, though. I had a horrible streak of pure mischief in me, and I just couldn't stay out of trouble.

But I was also eager to learn and excel at whatever I did. All week I studied different and fascinating things. There were horsemanship and swimming lessons. We studied butterflies and insects. I understood that these studies were leading up to tests at the end of the week. These tests, if you passed them, would get you something called honors for something called Pathfinders. On the last Saturday night of camp they awarded the honors. I didn't get a single one, and I cried very bitterly in my tent that night.

CHAPTER FIVE

Violin Lessons or a Life of Crime?

School began again in the fall of 1981. May and I continued to attend Milwaukee Junior Academy. Bayba, our grandmother, came to live with us that year. Like my mother, she was a teacher. Sixty years old when she immigrated, Bayba quickly learned English and began to teach in the United States. She taught nearly ten years before retiring.

My parents learned that a famous violinist, Cyrus Forough, was coming to the Wisconsin Conservatory of Music. Through the Music for Youth Program, I was invited to audition for Mr. Forough. I know I may be a little biased, but in my opinion, he is one of the best violinists in the world, and had studied with both David Oistrakh, perhaps the greatest Russian violinist of all time, and Josef Gingold, a legendary teacher in the United States.

I was worried. What was I going to play for this great man? Because friends and church members knew that I played the violin, they had given our family many records. As soon as we could obtain a turntable, I began to play those records. I listened to all the great violinists, like David Oistrakh, Mischa Ellman, Yehudi Menuhin, Jascha Heifetz, and others. For the first time in my life, I heard many of the great violin concertos. I fell in love with the Beethoven Violin Concerto, and I learned to play it in concert. So, for Mr. Forough, I played the first movement of the Beethoven Concerto. He accepted me as a student on full scholarship. I was eleven years old.

At our first lesson he looked at me kindly and said, "Jaime, let's put the Beethoven Concerto away, because it's going to be many, many years before you will be ready to play that again." And he began to take me through training, scales, etudes, studies, pieces, and eventually, some concertos.

I knew that studying with this great violinist and teacher was a wonderful opportunity. In fact, our entire family was aware of all the tremendous blessings we had already received in America. Our parents often reminded us of our life in Cuba, and the hardships and persecution that we had left behind. They also reminded me of the many times the Lord had spared my life. I had been sick frequently that first hard winter in Wisconsin and my mother reminded me that I had had rheumatic fever only a few years before, and according to the doctors in Cuba, had a damaged heart as a result. She believed that I had been miraculously cured, and used this experience to urge me to better behavior, without much success.

Pipo was not content with our life, even though we were beginning to do a little better financially. He wanted to get involved in the Lord's work in some way again. We made several trips during the following year to Chicago, where we met some people and made some friends who advised us to move to this city.

Mima had been a teacher in Cuba, prior to my birth, and she began to inquire about the steps needed to obtain a teaching certificate. Early in 1983, when I was twelve, she moved to Chicago to obtain her temporary teaching certificate. Miraculously, through the help of a Christian man who worked with the Illinois Board of

Education, her Cuban teaching certificate was recognized and validated. The Board issued her a full teaching certificate for the state of Illinois, and she started work as a teacher, earning a good income. She stayed on in Chicago for the next four months, while the rest of our family continued to live in Milwaukee.

In the summer of 1983, Pipo was offered a pastorate in Chicago, and we all moved to the city. Pipo started work part time as an associate pastor of the Humboldt Park Spanish Church, and part time as a literature evangelist among the Hispanic people of the Chicago area. The senior pastor, Oliver Mastrapa, had been a colleague of Pipo's in Cuba. We were happy to reunite our two families, and both my parents enjoyed their new jobs tremendously.

Humboldt Park was a dangerous section of the city, in the central part of Chicago—a mostly Hispanic neighborhood notorious for crime and gang warfare. Two rival gangs, the Latin Kings and the Disciples, were fighting for control of the area. We had to be careful about the color clothing we wore, because if you wore the yellow and black of the Latin Kings, the Disciples would attack you. Pipo's church was located in this part of town, however, we settled into a rented house to the north of Humbolt Park, where it was a little safer.

As soon as we arrived, our parents enrolled May and me in North Shore Junior Academy on the north side of the city. Dad bought a newer used car, a huge Plymouth that seemed like a brand-new Cadillac to us. Every morning, we would all pile into the car, and Pipo would drop Mima at her school, then drive May and me to school, before going on to his work. He would repeat the same routine in the afternoon.

So there I was in eighth grade at North Shore Junior Academy, learning a new school and getting acquainted with new kids all over again. A short time after we moved to Chicago, we learned, to our amazement and delight, that Mr. Forough had moved to the Chicago area to teach at the North Shore Conservatory of Music, north of Chicago in Winnetka. I was able to take lessons from him once again. How fortunate I've been to have had two of the greatest violin teachers in the world—Adolfo Guimbarda in Cuba from ages five to ten, and Cyrus Forough, from age eleven until the present. The importance of continuity with good teachers is invaluable for any young musician, and the Lord has blessed me greatly in that respect.

About this time, I took up a new instrument, the baritone saxophone, and began to play it in the band at North Shore Junior Academy. I had always wanted to play the trumpet, but for some reason Mima thought it would be hard on my lungs. Nobody else in the school wanted to play the huge baritone sax, so it became my band instrument of choice. I also began singing in the choir. My high-pitched voice earned me the unenviable position of being the only boy in the alto section, and I took a lot of teasing from my classmates for that, but I enjoyed singing very much.

I had a great time in eighth grade. My English had progressed to the point where I was comfortable with my teachers and my friends. However, my youthful exuberance and my tendency to get into trouble just seemed to increase. I fell in with some classmates who were daring and defiant. I thought they were cool, and wanted to be like them, so I got into the habit of stealing.

There was a candy store called Dolmar's across from the school, and at first it was a novelty to snitch a candy bar when you didn't have any money. Then it became a way to show off—something I could never resist. Somehow, when the temptation to steal came over me, I never thought about the consequences of being caught, or about the pain such behavior would cause Jesus, not to mention Mima and Pipo. I only thought about how clever and smart I was to get away with it. I could walk into Dolmar's and come out loaded down with candy bars and other treats and never be caught. My new friends applauded my success, and I basked in their praise, even though I knew very well that it was wrong. What I did not realize was how detrimental and hurtful this habit was going to become later in life.

My 8th grade graduation. That's Pipo, May, Mima, me, Leonel, and Bayba.

Summer 1982 at Camp Go Seek. That's my mom playing the accordion, me on the left, and my sister May on the right.

The beginning of my concert career in Chicago (1983).

My parents didn't need a rebellious and wayward teenager on their hands. They were both working hard. Both had two jobs. Mima taught school all day, and gave piano lessons afterwards. Even I began to take on violin students during my eighth-grade year. At one point, I had about twenty students. We formed a little string group and played in different churches in the area. I also performed as a soloist, and acquired a taste for applause. With my own lessons, my orchestra work, my students, and performances, I was very involved with music. I still hated practicing the violin, however!

One day, figuring I was old enough to make my own decisions, I announced to my parents that I intended to stop playing. "I'm sorry, Jaimito," Pipo said. "We are not going to allow you to stop playing the violin." Miserably, I accepted his decision and continued to practice and take lessons. Now, I'm so thankful for my parents' persistence!

My antisocial behavior continued. I began cheating. Unfortunately, I was good at it. Sadly, over the next few years I perfected my techniques, and often cheated when I didn't need to. Again, I did it for the thrill of getting away with something I knew very well was wrong. I was caught a couple of times during that school year, however.

Once in Bible class, I had taped some texts that we were supposed to have memorized, to the inside of my jacket. I took the test with the help of my secretly stashed notes, and turned in my paper. When I went outside to play, I left that jacket behind, and somehow it wound up on the floor. The teacher picked it up, and noticed the texts taped inside. She called my parents immediately. Once again, poor Mima and Pipo had to go to bat for their wayward son. I got into a great deal of trouble because of that incident, but regretfully, it didn't cure me of cheating.

Musically, however, I was making good progress. Ever since we had immigrated to the United States, I had been playing on borrowed or rented violins. Now my parents decided that it was time for me to have a violin of my own. In the spring of 1984, on the advice of my violin teacher, they took me to see a world-renowned violin maker named Carl Becker. I played several different violins, and we selected one. It wasn't a Carl Becker violin. It would be several more years before I was to own one of this great master's beautiful instruments. It was a special violin, however. My parents made a great sacrifice for me, spending $1700 on this violin and several hundred dollars more for a bow and a case. I played it in public for the first time at my eighth-grade graduation, a moment I'll always remember as one of the proudest of my life.

North Shore Junior Academy offered ten grades, and so I continued my education there. I had a wonderful and funny teacher in the ninth grade. His name was Eugene Baroya, but we called him Doc. His teaching style was much more free-spirited than that of any teacher I had had before. He loved algebra and computers, and we students loved him. Unfortunately, I was to let him down badly because of my bad behavior.

Near the end of my ninth-grade year, Doc took the ninth- and tenth-grade Economics classes on a field trip to Woodfield Mall. Our assignment was to shop for Doc's list of items, and to stay within his budget. The mall was located some distance from our school, and we traveled there together on the city bus. Once there, Doc allowed us to go our separate ways, with instructions to meet at a certain time and place to catch the bus for home.

I strolled into a music store with one of my friends. He saw a cassette tape by a group he liked. "I'd really like to have that cassette," he said.

I owed him some money, so I said, "If I steal it for you, will that make us even?"

"Sure," he said, grinning slyly.

I thought my stealing skills were highly developed. I knew just what to do. I picked up the cassette, which was in a large plastic case meant to discourage stealing, and took it over to a section of the store where records were displayed. Hiding the cassette down between the records, I managed to pry it loose from the case. I left the case with the records, and slipped the cassette into the inside pocket of my jacket. Proud of my skillful thievery technique, I stuck my hands in my jeans pockets and followed my friend out of the store.

The store manager followed and tapped me on the shoulder. "I think you have something that belongs to us," he said firmly. I wanted to die. I took the cassette out of my jacket pocket and handed it to the man, hoping he would let me leave, but he said, "I think you had better come back into the store with me. We have to call the police."

As I walked with him to the back of the store, I was shaking all over. "Please don't call the police," I begged. "If you just let me leave, I promise I'll never do this again. I'll pay for the cassette. I'll do whatever you want. Just, please, please don't call the police."

He shook his head and picked up the phone. Time moved extremely slow as he first tried to call the administrative offices of the mall, and then the mall security office. Each time he failed to connect with anybody, I breathed a sigh of relief. Next, however, he dialed the police department. I grew even more agitated and pleaded with him to let me leave. He would have none of it.

The police officer arrived and escorted me to the squad car. I was dying inside, shaking all over, filled with shame and fear. The officer must have taken some pity on me, because he said, "Normally I would handcuff you, but you don't look like the other kids I see who do this kind of thing on a regular basis. You don't look like a bad kid. I'm ashamed for you, that a nice kid like you would do something like this."

I was ashamed too, and terribly frightened. What would my parents do this time? What would they think of me? What about the other kids and Doc? What would they say when they learned about this?

Since I was only fourteen years old, the police didn't actually arrest me. I was taken to the police station, where I was asked more questions while an official filled out papers. They told me that because I was so young, there would be no permanent criminal record. Then they called my parents and asked them to come pick me up.

The policeman escorted me to a waiting room, closed the door and turned off the lights. I wept there, bitterly. I knew I had done something very wrong, and I was sorry. Unfortunately, my remorse wasn't real. I was sorry about getting caught and worried about what others would think of me.

I waited in that cold, dark room alone for several hours. Finally, my parents came. When I saw the pain and disappointment on their dear, tired faces, it was the greatest punishment I had ever received. I knew then how much I had hurt them. And I knew it wasn't the first time. For just a moment, looking into my parents' sad eyes, those early teachings of Jesus and His love flooded into my heart, and I knew how Jesus must feel, every time we disappoint Him.

I thought I would receive an intense talking-to, followed by a severe punishment. I knew I definitely deserved both. Incredibly, however, my parents never said a word to me during the entire trip home. This caused me to do some serious thinking on my own in the back seat of the car. Unfortunately, it wasn't serious enough, because I would steal again, later.

It didn't take long for the school officials to find out what had happened. I was suspended. The school board met to decide whether to allow me to finish the last few weeks of the school year. At least one member of the board argued that I should be expelled right then and there. Again, my poor parents were subjected to humiliation. They had to go before the school board and answer questions. I, too, was called to appear before the board. All my teachers and some of the people from the church were there. I was trembling from head to foot. I liked being the center of attention, but not this way! "Tell us why you shouldn't be expelled," the chairman asked.

I felt so ashamed, so humiliated. I said a quick silent prayer and then made a short, shaky speech, asking for their understanding and mercy, and pleading for another chance. When my speech was over, they asked me to wait outside while they deliberated. A few minutes later, I learned that they had voted to allow me to finish the year. Later I was to learn that God had used two special people,

Assir DaSilva and Johne Perlick, to intervene with the rest of the school board on my behalf. I'll always be immensely grateful to both of them. Johne, in particular, became a long-time friend who has helped me many, many times since. Once again, just like the time I had fallen off the roof as a child, God in His mercy had rescued me from my own foolishness.

Although I was going to be allowed to finish ninth grade and return for my tenth grade year, the school board made it clear that I would be on a probationary status. One slip-up, and there would be a warning letter to my parents. Another slip-up, and I would be out. I wish I could say I changed my ways. I got through the tenth grade without being expelled, but it was more by the grace of God than because of any improvement on my part.

During the summers following ninth and tenth grades, I worked as a student literature evangelist. Pipo ran a program for student LEs during these summers, bringing kids from Montemorelos University in Mexico on temporary work visas to work in Chicago's Spanish-speaking neighborhoods, and giving them an opportunity to earn tuition money. He suggested that I work with them, and paired me up with one of the younger students.

Funny thing, even though I was a clown and a showoff in school, I was shy in other situations, and found selling books difficult at first. I worked hard during that summer, getting up every morning at dawn and working late into the evening. I did well. The next summer, I asked Pipo to let me work on the student LE team again. The experience of selling Christian books and magazines was good for me and helped me mature in some ways, although I still had lots more growing up to do.

In 1987, my parents bought a house on the west side of Chicago. I was ready to start the eleventh grade. Because of my violin lessons and ever-growing performance schedule, my parents decided that I should not go away to Broadview Academy, a nearby boarding school, where many of my classmates planned to attend. I began to attend Chicago Christian Academy for my last two years of high school. The Good Shepherd Bible Church, affiliated with the Assemblies of God, ran this school, and Mima and Pipo believed it would be a good place for May and me.

I wish I could tell you that I changed my ways during my junior year. Sad to say, however, things got worse. I continued stealing. Even the memory of my experience in the police station didn't outweigh the thrill of getting away with stealing something, anything. I began to steal things that were bigger and more expensive. Inevitably, I would get caught again.

I had a little battery-powered portable TV that Pipo had gotten as a free gift. I watched it a lot—more than I should have. I loved watching Monday Night Football and other sporting events. Often I watched it late into the night after Mima and Pipo had gone to bed. Unfortunately, the thing used up batteries rapidly, and buying new ones was expensive. *I need some of those new rechargeable batteries,* I thought to myself.

I know you can tell where this story is going. But let me get it off my chest, anyway. I went to the grocery store on a Friday afternoon. Pedro Novales went with me that day. Pedro was a friend of the family. My parents had known him in Cuba, and had helped to bring him and his wife to the United States a short time before. Pedro was starting a brand new life in America.

As we walked into the store, I spied a display of rechargeable batteries. *Beautiful!* I thought. *Those are just what I need.* Pedro was looking at something else, so I quickly lined my pockets with the batteries. I was wearing pants with deep side pockets, and a couple of packs fit easily into each side. *Hah, I pulled that off easy!* I thought. You really couldn't see the batteries in my pockets at all, and since I had slipped them in so quickly and skillfully, I was sure I'd gotten away with it.

Pedro and I finished our shopping and made our way through the checkout. I grinned to myself as the batteries bumped against the sides of my legs with every step. Pedro was ahead of me as we walked out the door. Just as I thought I was safely out of the store, a security guard tapped me on the shoulder, and again I heard those dreaded words, "I think you have something that belongs to us."

He led me upstairs to the security office. I tried to give him the batteries, and pleaded with him to let me go. "Not so fast, young man," the guard growled. "I need to see some identification."

"I, I, I don't have any," I responded. "I'm only seventeen. I don't even have a driver's license yet."

"Well," the guard replied, "I'll need to speak to that man who was with you. If he can vouch for you and take you home, I will let you go. Otherwise, I'm going to have to take you to the police station."

Meanwhile, Pedro had come back into the store, looking for me. The guard had him brought to the office where I was being held. With great humiliation and embarrassment, I explained to this nice, Christian man, that I, the son of a minister, had been caught stealing.

By now, the security guard was wondering if Pedro was my accomplice. He looked from one of us to the other. "You two don't look like the kind of guys I usually catch at this kind of thing," he muttered, shaking his head in puzzlement. "You don't look like thieves, or gang members." He sighed and looked me in the eye. "I really don't know why you did this, but I'm going to have to tell your family," he said. He agreed to let us go if I gave him my father's name and phone number. Naturally, I hoped he would not call, but of course, he did, and told my dad the whole story.

I expected Pipo to punish me severely, to ground me for a long time at the very least. Instead, he spoke to me softly and gently, revealing the pain and sorrow my behavior had caused my mother and him. I knew I had disappointed him once again. As I saw the love and hurt in Pipo's eyes, I knew I had disappointed Jesus too. Slowly it was beginning to dawn on me that religion was not just a bunch of "do's" and "don'ts." I caught a glimpse then of how much God loved me, and realized that His law is love. Keeping God's commandments was something He wanted me to do for my own good and happiness. I decided then, in 1987, that with God's help, I was never going to steal again.

CHAPTER SIX

Music or Medicine

Throughout the last two years of high school, I continued to study the violin, and many more performing opportunities came my way. I played with the Waukegan Symphony Orchestra and the Classical Symphony, as well as with other orchestras, and I was invited to join the Chicago Civic Orchestra, which was the training ground for the Chicago Symphony Orchestra. I was gaining valuable experience as a principal violinist in the second violin section of an orchestra, or as an assistant concertmaster of another. During my junior year, I played several times at Orchestra Hall in Chicago, and later on at the world-renowned Carnegie Hall in New York with the New England Youth Ensemble. I was also doing a great deal of concertizing in churches—a natural for me, since I had grown up performing in church.

While still in high school, I recorded my first album. In my travels, I had re-connected with a man named David González, who worked for a children's program called *Your Story Hour*. His family had known mine in Cuba; in fact, we lived in the same neighborhood. David had promised me that he was going to help me record an album someday. He did, when I was seventeen! During my senior year, David invited me to come to *Your Story Hour*'s small recording facility in Berrien Springs, Michigan. With my friend Bryan Shilander accompanying me on the piano, and another friend, sound engineer Dan Baltazar running the session, we recorded a two-track live album of sacred pieces, which we called *Adoration*. We made the entire recording in about ten hours—an unbelievably short time, and it was released in the fall of 1987.

As I went from place to place performing, I realized that although people were kind and generous in their response when I played long concertos or my own adaptations and arrangements, the audience response was much greater when I played familiar hymns—the music they knew and loved—the music that spoke to their souls. Right from that first album, I decided that I was always going to record music that was spiritually meaningful and familiar to people.

Adoration was simple and humble. It did not cost very much to produce. In fact, David didn't charge me a penny for using *Your Story Hour*'s facilities. He just wanted to help me get started. He knew that making a first album is an important step in any music ministry, because albums can help get you known, and that leads to concerts. In addition, proceeds from an album's sale can help offset expenses, and if the artist is lucky, they can bring in a little income, too.

Making my first album was thrilling, but I had other things on my mind. As my senior year ended, it was time to consider my college education and future. As strange as it may seem, despite the joy of making an album and concertizing with symphony orchestras, I was not one bit interested in the further study of music. Even amid the growing expectations about my musical future, I had never really considered that I would make music my life's work. I was still sticking with a decision that I had made when I was six years old. I was determined to be a physician.

My parents supported me in this decision, even though I knew they had their own ambitions for me. Pipo cherished a hope that I

Family photo from 1988

After a concert in Orchestra Hall in Chicago (1986). I played in the Classical Symphony Orchestra and joined the Civic Orchestra.

At a friend's wedding in 1984. Me, Mima, Pipo, and May.

would enter the ministry someday. I knew Mima wanted a musical career for me, and always had.

I talked with my friend, Bryan Shilander, an accomplished and well-known pianist and the assistant dean at Chicago Musical College of Roosevelt University, with whom I had performed on several occasions. He, along with my violin teacher, urged me to try music. "You're at a crossroads," Bryan told me. "When I was at that point in my life, I decided to give music a chance. And here I am."

But I was dead set against music as a career. Strangely enough, I disliked everything about music—everything, that is, except performing. I loved the feeling I got when people responded to my performances. However, I still hated practicing. I only did it to be good enough to perform. I was bound and determined to be a doctor.

As I pondered where to go to college, my first thought, of course, was that I wanted to go to a Christian school. I had some good opportunities to do just that. Andrews University and Loma Linda University, for example, both offered me scholarships. However, they were contingent on my majoring in music.

For several reasons, I wound up at Loyola University in Chicago in the fall of 1988, majoring in biology. It was and is a fine school with an excellent academic reputation. It was also close to home. In addition, they offered me the best financial aid package of any school where I had applied, and that was important to my family and me.

When I first started at Loyola, my schedule was so full that I thought seriously about giving up the violin altogether. That first year of college was an eye-popping, overwhelming experience. Up to that point, I had attended small Christian schools. Loyola was big! It had 15,000 students, and I didn't know a single one of them. On registration day, I showed up at the main campus on the north side of Chicago—in a beautiful setting right along the lakeshore. Orientation was overwhelming and scary. However, I had learned a little bit about blending in since my earlier school days, so I trod lightly and tried to get to know the ropes. I felt my way around and got myself registered for courses. I had never felt so alone.

Expectations at Loyola were significantly different from high school. Nobody hounded you to do your homework or go to classes. If you didn't want to go, you didn't go. If you didn't want to study, that was your problem. I'm a born procrastinator, and without the familiar pressure from teachers, this freedom went straight to my head. I know now that many kids go through this when they start college, but I think I was worse than most. I would put off studying or not show up for class, only to have my grades reveal how poorly prepared I was. Then I would get serious and try to make up for lost time. This pattern of alternately slacking off and cramming did not improve until my last year of college, when I finally learned to discipline myself and study more consistently.

I got to know some of my instructors well. Mrs. Mary Spaeth was my English 101 teacher. Even though I was still having some trouble with English, I enjoyed her class tremendously. She was a warm and generous person who took the time to talk with me. I often visited her office, and we had long conversations. I shared my deep religious convictions with her. She was and is a deeply spiritual person, although, as she told me then, not a "religious" person. Of all my professors at Loyola, she is the only one with whom I have stayed in contact through the years. We continue to be good friends.

As I said, I didn't know anybody at Loyola. I went directly each day to Damen Hall, the building where the majority of my courses were held. Sometimes I would go to the gym after classes, and lift weights, or run. Often I would join in a pick-up game of basketball. Other than that, I had very little interaction with my fellow students.

The old habit of showing off was still alive and well in me, and in the few conversations I did have, I had managed to mention to several people that I drove a 'Vette. Since I always parked several blocks away from school, nobody had seen my 'Vette. I parked far away on purpose, because I didn't want them to find out that my 'Vette was not a Corvette, but a Chevette.

Somehow, somebody found out that I played the violin, and invited me to play at a meeting of the Spanish club. Some time afterwards, I got a phone call from a Loyola theology professor, a priest named Mike Notek.

"I hear you play the violin," he said. "I'd like you to play for our talent show."

"What talent show?" I asked.

"Oh, every year at Loyola we have a student talent show. It's part of a program called Hunger Week. We raise money for food and clothing for the poor," he responded. He told me more about the talent show, and that lots of students participated.

I protested that it didn't sound like an event where classical music would be welcome, but the priest was very persuasive. *Well, why not?* I thought. *Nobody knows me anyway. It could be a way to meet people.* So I agreed to play. I chose a piece that I thought a group of students would like, and I began to practice it.

The night of the talent show was the first Thursday in November 1988. I came home from school and dressed for the concert. The weatherman on the radio was predicting cold, windy weather for that night, so I dressed warmly, including a heavy wool sweater. As I got into my car, I realized that the temperature had indeed dropped. I turned on the radio, and the announcer said, "Folks, we call Chicago the windy city. Tonight it is certainly living up to its name. It is extremely windy and cold out there. The wind-chill factor is going to make it feel like 20 or 30 degrees below. Stay inside if you can."

I shivered inside my several layers of clothing and turned on the heater. Once I assured myself that the heater was working, I stood my violin up in its case on the passenger seat, strapped it in with the seat belt, and took off for Loyola. As I drove, I thought about the program—picturing what it would be like, what the other musicians might play. Loyola was an elite university. So at least some of it would be highbrow stuff. I hoped they'd accept what I planned to play. I was nervous about what my fellow students would think of my playing and me.

I arrived at the campus, and found a parking spot near the auditorium. As I got out of the car and picked up my violin, I quickly glanced around to be sure none of the students I'd bragged to about my 'Vette were in the vicinity. I didn't notice anybody looking at me, so I walked up the steps and into the building where the auditorium was.

There was a buzz of anticipation in the hall. People were running around making last-minute adjustments to the sound and lighting. Hundreds of seats faced the front. Bright spotlights with colored gels focused on the stage. Huge speakers stood on either side at the front, and on the stage itself, there were at least a dozen microphones, as well as electric guitars and drums. At the back of the auditorium, two sound engineers wearing headphones were fiddling with a large console.

I located a program, and found my name in the lineup. I would be playing in the first half. I took the cassette with my background accompaniment to one of the engineers. I met Mike Notek. He introduced me to the master of ceremonies. I gave him my name, and told him how to pronounce it. Then I sat down near the front. Then I got up and walked around the auditorium. Then I sat down again. I was more anxious and nervous than I had ever been at a performance. I looked around at the seats. Only a few were filled. Maybe nobody would show up. I relaxed a little. Then students began pouring into the auditorium, and around 7:30, the program started to a packed and rowdy house—many of them wild-looking teenagers with ripped clothes and dyed hair—every person there obviously ready to have a good time.

As the program began, I realized that this show was presented repeatedly year after year, with a handful of the performers participating in it annually. The Chemistry Department professors did a barbershop quartet sing-along. Other faculty members performed as well, but student rock bands performed most of the numbers. The whole thing was very informal, the students in the audience often joking with each other and doing their own thing during the performances. At times, the audience was unmerciful. One of the staff writers of the university paper got up to do a comedy routine, and the crowd booed him off the stage.

This isn't a good idea, I thought to myself about forty-five minutes into the program. *This isn't my kind of show. I need to get out of here.* Since he had printed my name in the program, I decided I needed to let the professor who had recruited me know I had changed my mind.

"You know," I said, when I had located him back stage, "I just don't feel very comfortable playing here tonight."

He just looked at me. "Why not?" he asked.

"Well, I play classical violin, and all the music I've heard so far tonight is pretty far from classical. I don't think the students are going to appreciate it. I think it would just be better if I didn't play."

"Look," he said. "It's going to be OK. In fact, being different and playing a different kind of music could just work to your advantage."

I thought about the comedian who was booed off the stage. He was different too. "Maybe next year," I said.

"Well," he replied with a sigh. "Of course, you can do whatever you want. However, you promised me that you were going to play. Your name is in the program. I'm asking you not to let me down."

I had no answer for that. By then, it was nearly time for my turn, so I went back stage, took my violin out of the case, and tried to warm up. I was so nervous that I was having trouble breathing. My hands were shaking. They were cold, yet they were sweating. I tried to take a few deep breaths to relax, as the band that was performing ahead of me cleared off the stage. I saw the master of ceremonies come up to the microphone to introduce me.

I bowed my head. *Lord, I have no idea what I'm doing in this place tonight,* I prayed. *It's obvious I'm different from the rest of these kids. If I am going to be different, please help me to be different for You. Please help me to be a light and an example for You.* As I opened my eyes, I felt a little better, but I was still nervous.

I had asked the master of ceremonies to introduce me as "Jamie George." Of course, my name is written and pronounced Jaime Jorge in Spanish. However, when I arrived in the United States, I realized how difficult it was for Americans to say the Spanish pronunciation, so I had translated my name to English. Jaime became Jamie, and Jorge became George. By this time, everybody called me Jamie George, and that is how I had asked the master of ceremonies to introduce me. For some reason, however, this good man decided to try to pronounce my name in Spanish.

"Ladies and gentlemen," he began, "it's my pleasure to introduce our next participant this evening. Now, we're doing lots of different kinds of music here tonight, and next we have a violinist. He's going to come out here and do a solo for you, so put your hands together and give a warm welcome to *Hymee Horgee!*"

I don't know how that sounds to you as you read it, but when it came out of that man's mouth, I wanted to crawl into a hole and never come out. At the sound of that name, the crowd, which had been loud and boisterous, became suddenly quiet. Evidently, they had never heard such an ugly name before.

What in the world is a Hymee Horgee? I thought wildly. I had been secretly hoping that this concert was going to be my opportunity to meet some people—maybe some girls, even—and now this horrible man had ruined it for me. I felt very embarrassed. I wanted to run out of the building and never come back. But there wasn't anywhere for me to run. I was right behind the master of ceremonies—the spotlight was waiting for me. I couldn't do anything but go out there and begin playing my song. As I walked out onto the stage, the quiet continued. Everybody was curious to see what this person with the weird name looked like.

As I reached the microphone, I looked out at the audience. I was dressed in a sweater and slacks, and I knew I looked clean-cut and neat. I also knew I looked hopelessly out of place. I took the microphone. "Please hold off the tomatoes," I said. A laugh ran through the crowd. They thought I was joking, but I was serious. I couldn't bear to have my violin doused with a tomato or a rotten egg. Halloween had not been that long ago.

I put my violin up to my chin, closed my eyes, and began to play. The piece I had chosen was a passionate, romantic, intense composition entitled *Czardas,* by Monti. It started slow. I figured it would be boring for this crowd, but I just prayed they would stay with me until I got to the fast part. I was hoping they would like that better. The music got livelier. I kept my eyes closed, but I began to feel that the audience was with me. The piece got faster and faster. Then it slowed again. In the next section I played harmonics—beautiful soft notes—then more fast playing right up to the end. The spotlight was hot. I was sweating profusely in my woolly sweater. I finished with an arpeggio, going from a low D up very high, and a big flourish. I finally opened my eyes, after four minutes of playing with my eyes closed. Instantly the sweat began running into them, and the bright spotlight blinded me. I couldn't look up, so all I could see were people's feet and legs. Suddenly, I saw all those feet and legs move. Everybody just jumped up.

Oh, no! I said to myself. *This is worse than I thought. They're going to come up on the stage and just kill me right here.* Then I realized that when they stood up, their legs did not move. Then their hands came together and I heard the most thunderous applause I had ever heard in my life. Students were yelling and screaming, clapping and jumping up and down. It was amazing.

They liked it! I thought. I started to smile and relax a little. I walked to one side of the stage and took a bow, and then moved to the other side of the stage and took another bow. I walked off the stage, and still they didn't stop. People backstage said to me, "You gotta go back out there. They're not done. Get back out there again."

When I came back out again for a curtain call, the applause continued. Then they started chanting my name: "Hy-mee Hor-gee, Hy-mee Hor-gee!" I didn't know whether to laugh or cry. Suddenly I was having a great time. I started waving at people, singling out certain ones here and there for a special little salute. I could hardly believe what was happening.

I sat through the rest of the program in a daze, just waiting for it to be over. I wanted to get home and tell my parents. It was nearly midnight when I returned to my 'Vette, climbed in, strapped in my violin, and turned on the heat.

I was still so excited that I yelled and screamed all the way home, frequently throwing my clenched fist up in the air. My sweaty exuberance fogged up all the windows. I flew through the near-empty midnight streets of Chicago, eager to tell my dad what had happened.

I jumped the seven steps to my front door in one leap, carrying my violin. Inside, I put the case down on the nearest chair and let out my biggest celebratory yell yet. "Yes!" I shouted into the darkness. Immediately I heard a loud thump coming from my parents' bedroom. "What was that?" I thought, fear suddenly replacing elation. Maybe there was a burglar in the house. Pipo was home alone. Mima had gone to Miami to visit family. Quickly I crossed to their room and opened the door. Pipo was slowly getting up from the floor, looking dazed. My shout had awakened him from a deep sleep, and startled, he had fallen out of bed.

"Pipo, what are you doing down there?" I asked, helping him up. "Oh, well, never mind, I have this great story to tell you." My dad listened as kindly as possible, and then suggested that I go to my room and get some sleep. I tried, but I didn't sleep much that night.

For several days afterwards, as I passed people in the hallways at school, they would recognize me. "Excuse me," they would say. "Aren't you Hymee Horgee? Aren't you the violinist who played in the talent show?" It was embarrassing, but I was pleased that people remembered me. It seemed that I was no longer anonymous.

In a way, that performance marked a turning point in my ongoing relationship with music—and not just because of the standing ovation. I was eighteen years old, and had struggled against my musical talent all my life. While I had always enjoyed being in front of people, I hated practicing so much that it often overcame the joy of performing. Over the next few days, as I pondered what had happened, I began to realize the incredible power of music, and the profound difference between good music and bad. I had seen the power of the good demonstrated that night in the students' reaction.

Humbly, I acknowledged that the Lord had blessed me because I had asked Him to let me be a light. For the first time, I began to acquire something of an adult perspective on my music as a ministry.

I started to think of my musical talent as a gift from God—one that I had a responsibility to use for Him to bring a blessing to others—and not simply as a chore being forced on me by my parents and teachers.

I have told the story of that concert at Loyola many times during my performances in recent years. One morning in 1998, ten years later, I told it as part of a service at the First Baptist Church in Longwood, Florida. Afterwards, as I was greeting people, I noticed a young woman standing on the edge of the group. She waited until everyone else was gone, and then she approached me.

"You don't know me, Jaime, but I remember you," she said.

"How is that?" I asked.

"I was in that student crowd at Loyola when you played the violin ten years ago. I was at a low point in my life that night. I had a brain tumor. It had caused me to go blind, and I was facing surgery the next day. The prognosis was not good. As I lay on the operating table that next morning prior to the anesthetic taking effect, all I could remember was the young man who had played the violin the night before. Something about him seemed so different from the rest of the students. I decided to pray. I said to the Lord, 'If You'll allow me to come out of this surgery alive, I would like to be different, too, like that young man.' "

Here she was, standing in front of me in church, ten years later, alive, well, and obviously alight with her love for the Lord. I was stunned. I had thought being called Hymee Horgee was a humbling experience. But there is nothing so humbling as realizing that the Lord has used you to speak to someone else. I am convinced that He does use each of us that way. Through us, some people may see the glimpse of Jesus that will change their lives.

As I said, after that Loyola concert, I began to think much more seriously about my relationship with the Lord and the kind of music I should play in public. I had realized music's fantastic power. Sadly, that is not to say my life changed completely at that point. I was still immature, still too easily tempted into doing wrong, still unable to consistently serve the Lord or even look after my own best interests.

CHAPTER SEVEN

Life in the Spotlight

College continued—and overall, it was a good experience for me. I struggled with my grades. Let's face it—by now you know that I had never been an extremely disciplined person. My accomplishments up to that point in life were thanks to a God-given talent and a mother with an unbending will. In college, I didn't have Mima's kind of direct supervision, and so I continued in an unhealthy pattern of alternately cramming and procrastinating. In addition, I tried to juggle my studies with my burgeoning musical career. By this time, I had recorded a couple of albums, and by the end of my sophomore year, I was traveling all over the country, giving concerts on most weekends. I was trying to serve two masters—my lifelong dream of being a doctor, and my music ministry, which seemed to have a life of its own.

In spite of all this uncertainty, I enjoyed my studies. During my second year, I took a Spanish Literature class from Dr. Miguel Martinez, a professor who had been teaching at Loyola for many years. We became good friends, and I spent a lot of time in his home in Chicago's northwest section. He was one of the most passionate and intelligent people I have ever known. He had an immense gift for teaching, engaging his students and urging them to analyze what they read, and to look beyond the plot or story line.

"What is really happening here?" he would ask the class as we analyzed a story. A student would raise his hand and mumble, "Well, I think this is what the author is trying to say—." Dr. Martinez would hold up his hand and shake his head. "Never apologize," he'd say. "When you say 'I think,' you're apologizing. You are saying, 'This is just my opinion and I'm sure it doesn't really matter very much.' Speak up—say what you think, and don't ever apologize for it!"

I learned much from Dr. Martinez, and remained close to him, even after college. Before he died, God gave me the opportunity to share my love for Jesus with him, and I believe I will see him again in heaven.

Loyola also taxed me in ways other than academically. My faith and my religious convictions were sorely tested. Slowly I was coming to realize that my beliefs and standards needed to grow out of a personal relationship with the Lord, not just my parents' teachings.

Unfortunately, before that spiritual awakening occurred, I was tempted into participating in some of the secular activities of my peers and classmates. Prior to college, I had never been inside a nightclub. I had never drunk an ounce of alcohol. Now I began to experiment, in an offhand way, with these things. I hated the taste of beer, but I decided to drink a little, because everybody else was doing it. I went clubbing with my friends occasionally—coming home at two in the morning. My careful upbringing and God's grace saved me from immersing myself in these activities, however. Staying in a nightclub drinking until the early hours of the morning struck me as meaningless and worthless. I realized that spending my life that way would be a royal waste of time—but still I indulged in it from time to time.

The thing that saved me from sinking into a life of booze and nightclubbing was the ministry of music. The more I traveled and played, the more opportunities came my way. By 1990, I had recorded three albums. Oh, they weren't elaborate expensive projects, but they went a long way toward helping me get established, and they helped to pay the bills.

My two masters were getting more and more demanding. I know now why the Lord says we can't serve two masters because for those last years of college, that's exactly what I was doing.

On the weekends, I would use my musical talent to get people's attention. Then I would speak to them and share my faith. On Monday, I would be back at college—slipping into the bad habits again, doing things I knew I should not be doing as a Christian. Despite the fact that I knew better, I enjoyed the pleasure and excitement of doing these untried things, of making new friends.

About this time, I got involved with a girl I met at school, and let our relationship go further than it should have. I knew it was wrong, but like the other temptations I had succumbed to, it was exciting. Little did I know how much pain and heartache this particular temptation was to cause me in years to come. We broke up after dating for a couple of years. During the rest of my college years and beyond, I drifted in and out of several relationships with girls I met at school and elsewhere. I was insecure and confused when it came to matters of the heart. I wound up hurting others, and myself, more than once. I'd meet a girl, become infatuated with her, lead her on, and then realize that it wasn't the real thing at all. Then I'd have a lot of apologizing and backtracking to do.

As in so many other areas of my life, I failed to seek the Lord's help in helping me to establish healthy relationships with members of the opposite sex. Even though I asked Him to help me choose the right person to be my life's mate, I still fell into temptation. I think, during those last years of college, I was spiritually sleepwalking—talking the talk, but not really walking the walk.

After concerts, people would come up and talk to me. They would compliment me on my playing, and thank me for my witness—for the testimony I had given. Young people in particular would say,

"Man, you're so young and you've got your stuff together so well. Your life is an inspiration!"

I would smile and nod, but inside I would feel like a fake. Even when I was involved in doing the things I knew I shouldn't, I still felt the tugs of conscience. I still remembered the tenderness and love of my parents and the teachings they had instilled in me. It amazed and humbled me that somehow God was allowing my music to be used for His glory, even though I knew I was not living up to His principles.

I was quickly becoming accustomed to life in the spotlight. Unfortunately, it went to my head. I grew to enjoy being in the limelight very much—to need it. I was a cocky teenager, appeared to be very self-confident and assured, on the outside at least. People loved me and wanted to be around me. I thought I could do anything. I played for mayors, governors, dignitaries, and heads of state. My own head swelled and I became puffed up and arrogant.

All the travel I was doing led to some interesting incidents— several of which involved my violin. You will remember that first violin my parents purchased for me in 1984, not long after we came to the United States. Let me tell you what happened to it. One evening in 1987 when I was in high school, I was rehearsing with the Roosevelt University Orchestra in downtown Chicago. I was exhausted when I arrived at this rehearsal, because it had followed days of exams during which I had not eaten or slept much. During the rehearsal, I threw my head back to relax my neck a little. Somehow, this cut off the circulation of blood to my brain, and I had a seizure. I pitched forward off my chair, and as I fell to the floor, my knee went through my violin, shattering it in a hundred pieces.

Unfortunately, that violin wasn't insured. My parents, at huge sacrifice, replaced it with an even better violin that cost $3,300. A couple of years later, in 1989, thanks to the generous assistance of friends and supporters, I was able to purchase a beautiful instrument made by the great Carl Becker. It was worth more than $20,000. That may sound like a lot, but to put it in perspective, the greatest violins in the world today, such as a Stradivarius or a Guarnerius, cost as much as $3,000,000.

Even though it wasn't a Strad, I treated this violin like a member of the royal family. I guarded it with my life, almost never letting it out of my sight. In fact, I still treat it that way. However, that violin, too, has had a couple of narrow escapes. I remember one occasion when I made a trip to Green Bay, Wisconsin. The concert was planned for the following evening, but I had been asked to play for church in the morning. So I needed to leave early Saturday morning. Now, I am not a morning person, so I had packed the car the night before with my clothes, the albums I was taking along to sell, and the directions I needed to find the concert location. Oh, I was really organized. Right before I went to bed, I placed my precious violin right next to my bed, so I would not even think of forgetting it.

Next morning, I got up, threw on my clothes, and hit the road by 5:00 A.M. Along the way, I listened to the Moody Bible Institute radio station out of Chicago, whistling and humming to keep myself awake. I arrived in Green Bay at the church where I was to perform by 9:30 A.M. I parked the car, turned off the ignition, and reached over to the passenger seat to pick up my violin. As you know, that's where it usually travels, strapped in with the seat belt like a passenger. Not there. In the four hours I'd been driving, I hadn't noticed that it wasn't there. I looked in the back seat. Not there. *I never put my violin in the trunk,* I thought to myself, but I looked anyway. Not there. *Lord,* I prayed, *please help me. Forgive me for forgetting my violin, and help me figure out how to get it back in time.*

Comforted by my prayer, but still worried down to the soles of my shoes, I did a quick mental calculation of the traveling time it would take me to turn around and head back to Chicago to get my instrument. *If I leave right now,* I thought, *I'll be home by 1:30 P.M. Then if I turn right around again, I could be back by 6:00 P.M. The concert is supposed to start at 7:00 P.M. I don't have a whole lot of time, but I think I can make it. I'd better go inside and let the pastor know that I won't be playing special music this morning.* The greeter at the door recognized me immediately, grabbed my hand and shook it vigorously.

"Welcome, Jaime! We're so glad to have you, and we're all looking forward to your special music this morning," she said, pumping my hand up and down.

"Um," I replied. "Do you think I could speak to the pastor?"

"Sure," she said, frowning slightly, and went to get him.

"Pastor, I have a problem," I said when the good man approached me.

"Jaime, what is it? We are so glad you're here. How can we help you?"

"I left my violin at home," I replied miserably. I was nineteen years old, and it was one of the most embarrassing moments of my life—and as you know by now, I've had a lot of them. The minister's face reflected his consternation. I was sure he was thinking, *What is this kid's problem? How could he show up without his instrument?*

"Look, pastor," I said. "I think I can drive home and pick it up and get back in time for the concert tonight."

"Wait a minute," he said, his face brightening. "There's a little girl in our church who started taking violin lessons not too long ago. You could use her violin!"

I tried to explain to him that I probably would not be able to play a violin so much smaller than mine. Besides, I wanted my own violin! It is very difficult to play another instrument on the spur of the moment when you haven't had time to get to know it or practice with it. However, the minister thought he had come up with a brilliant idea. Now other people were gathering around, hearing the story, and offering their advice and suggestions. Talk about an awkward situation! They were all amazed that the "famous" Jaime Jorge had shown up to play without his violin!

Just then, a man spoke to me quietly. "I heard about your little problem," he smiled. I thought he was making fun of me. However, he continued, "Why don't you try out this girl's violin, play one song on it for special music this morning? If it turns out that you don't like it—if you can't play it, maybe I can do something to help you get your violin."

I looked at him, my thoughts churning. Was he pulling my leg? Did he have an airplane or something? Was he planning to fly me to Chicago? I was skeptical, but I agreed to play the small violin for church. It was obvious that I was not going to be able to play an entire concert on it. Afterwards, he came up to me again.

"OK," he said. "After lunch we'll take my plane and go get your violin." So after a leisurely potluck lunch with the church members, we called my parents and asked them to meet us at Midway Airport. Then Scott Davis and I boarded his single-engine two-seater Cessna and took off for Chicago. It was my first time in a private plane. We flew most of the way over Lake Michigan. I was exhilarated, but also scared. *If I sneeze,* I thought, *this plane is going to go into the lake, and I don't know how to swim.*

We arrived at Midway, where my parents were waiting. We collected the violin, turned right around, and flew back to Green Bay, returning in plenty of time for the concert.

I have never forgotten to take my violin to a concert with me since then. I have forgotten other things, but never my violin. It's a good thing, too, because I have never come across another pilot who was willing to fly me back home to get it.

I did almost lose my violin another time, however. It was in 1991 at the height of the Gulf War. I was at O'Hare Airport in Chicago, standing in line to get a ticket changed. Needing to free my hands to deal with the paperwork, I set the violin down beside me in the line. I worked my way to the front of the line, changed my ticket, and went home. About an hour and a half later, I was relaxing on the couch, watching a Chicago Bulls basketball game on TV, when I remembered my violin. Frantically, I threw myself in my car and drove to the airport, praying all the way, thinking surely it had been stolen or confiscated by then, but when I got to the line where I had waited before, the violin was sitting exactly where I had left it. Once again, the Lord had shown me His magnificent love.

Still, in spite of these evidences of God's caring, I continued to try to serve God and Mammon. I wanted to get as much fun as possible out of the things that this world had to offer—and yet I wanted to be faithful and obedient to the Lord. Obviously, that was not going to work.

As I mentioned, I had recorded three albums by 1990. Dr. Elvin Rodriguez, an extraordinary pianist, had accompanied me on the last two. In 1991, when I asked him to help me with a fourth album, he was not available, so I looked around for someone who could help me with the producing and arranging.

I turned to my good friend Pastor Dan Pabón, who had already helped me in so many ways, by setting up the recording studios for the previous two albums, assisting with bookings, and otherwise representing me in my music ministry. Dan called up a friend of his, Mick Thurber, a pastor and musician who lived in southern California. Mick couldn't help either, but recommended a young man named Paul Tucker. Paul agreed to take on the job, and we set a date to begin the recording.

A couple of weeks later, I walked into his studio in Riverside, California to meet him and his twin brother, Stephen. When I arrived to begin the project, I thought I knew all there was to know about recording. After all, I was a veteran with three albums under my belt. In two weeks we had completed my fourth album, *You'll Never Walk Alone,* and I had learned so much that I felt unworthy to be in the same room with Paul and Stephen. They are two of the finest musicians, among the greatest talents I have ever known. Since we began our working relationship, we have recorded five albums together.

You'll Never Walk Alone was the last album I recorded before finishing college. I continued to concertize during the last couple of years of college, but as I faced those last few semesters of school, I knew I was going to need to devote more time to my studies. I also knew that I had to prepare for the Medical College Admissions Test or MCAT exam, which would determine whether I would be accepted into medical school.

CHAPTER EIGHT

A Time of Testing

Something strange started to happen to me in the early spring of 1990, during my sophomore year of college. I developed a most peculiar illness. I first noticed that something unusual was happening to my forehead. A thin red line ran vertically from my hairline down to the middle of my right eyebrow. I ignored it at first—but it didn't go away. After a few weeks, the line got thicker, and still thicker. It appeared to me, as I peered anxiously into the mirror, that something was eating away my forehead. The line soon became two lines; one on the left and one on the right side. The area in between was turning hard, becoming unpigmented and dead-looking.

I was getting alarmed. I needed to look good, and here was this "thing" on my forehead that looked horrible. The thin façade of my self-confidence began to crumble.

I went to my mother. "There's something strange happening to my forehead," I told her. She took one look and made an appointment with our doctor. He did not know what was wrong with me, but sent me to a plastic surgeon to see if there was anything he could do. The plastic surgeon was baffled, and suggested I see a dermatologist. Uncle Leonel, who by now had graduated from medical school and was working at the Jackson Memorial Hospital at the University of Miami, got me an appointment with a dermatologist there named Dr. Vincent Falanga.

Dr. Falanga examined me carefully. Then he brought in a couple of interns to have a look. Finally, he said, "You have an illness called linear scleroderma. I'm going to put you on some medication."

My hopes rose. Finally, I had found somebody who knew what I had and what to do about it. "How do we cure this thing?" I asked.

"We don't," he replied. "There is no known cure, but we can start you on some medications which we hope will mask this illness."

He explained to me that scleroderma is an autoimmune disease. The body's immune system is a powerful agent that enables us to fight disease, but sometimes our own immune system can attack us. That is what was happening in my case. There is no known cause for this disease, and no cure.

However, one of the possible triggers, according to Dr. Falanga, was stress. Well, I certainly had enough of that. In addition to going to college full time and traveling nearly every weekend to perform one or more concerts, I had accumulated a huge load of debt, partly due to the albums I had recorded. If stress was a trigger, I qualified. Still, I wondered, *Why me?* Dr. Falanga told me that there were only 750 known cases of this disease in the United States. Why was I singled out?

Dr. Falanga prescribed three different medications, an antibiotic, an anti-inflammatory drug, and a cortizone steroid called Prednisone. He did not offer much more information, other than to tell me I would have to take these drugs on a daily basis for several years.

I was in despair. I hated what I saw when I looked in the mirror. This horrific illness appeared to be eating the skin, the tissue, the muscle, and even the bone of my skull, down through the right side

The ravages of linear scleroderma. The disease and the side effects of the medication left me at an all-time emotional low.

of my nose and around the cheek area under my eye. I could literally see the disease eating away at my face. I became very bitter. I was angry with God. At that point, I have to admit, I was mostly worried about my looks. Although I was not aware of it at the time, I learned later that the systemic form of scleroderma can be fatal, and often a localized case, like mine, could become systemic.

I started taking my medications—hoping that they would reverse the damage already done to my face. Nobody prepared me for the side effects. The Prednisone, in particular, affected me profoundly. I broke out in hives on my face, neck, and chest. I had mood swings, going from lows with complete loss of energy and lack of motivation, to uncontrollable highs. I couldn't cope with my daily activities, and spent a lot of time sleeping. I would come home from my classes at 6:00 P.M. and go straight to bed. Next morning I would get up, go to school, come home, and go right to bed again. The worst part was that, despite the medication and its side effects, the disease wasn't slowing down.

Then the worst side effect set in. Prednisone can make your joints and tissue swell. I developed a round moon face. I gained a tremendous amount of weight. With my big round face, and the huge indentation in my forehead, I thought I looked like an accident victim who had run into a light pole. I was at an all-time emotional low. I was unhappy, insecure, ashamed of my appearance, and bitter towards God.

Month after month, I traveled to Miami to see Dr. Falanga. He would examine me, call in more physicians, shake his head, and tell me to continue the medication. Nothing seemed to change. Both the disease and the medication's side effects continued. I had no energy. Life had lost its zest. I was an angry and frustrated person.

During this time, my focus was entirely on myself. I was worried about what I looked like now, and what I might be going to look like for the rest of my life. I went through the motions of my usual busy and stressful life—going to class all week and concertizing every weekend—but inside I was broken and empty. I was angry with God. On the outside I tried to put up a good front, but inside I was struggling with deep feelings of ugliness, inadequacy, and insecurity. By 1994, the ugliness appeared to be fading somewhat, and Dr. Falanga told me that he thought the illness had gone into remission. He told me to continue taking the steroids for another few months.

During this period, I was grateful to anyone who showed me the least attention or appreciation, especially if that person was a girl. This, combined with my usual impulsive behavior, led to more ill-advised relationships and further insecurity.

Despite all my problems, I managed to graduate from Loyola University in 1992 with a Bachelor of Arts degree. That fall I took the MCAT exam. Usually, this exam is taken during the junior year of a premedical course, but because I was following two career paths at once, I realized I needed more time. I decided to take a few months off after college, rest up and prepare for the exam, and then while waiting to learn whether I was going to be accepted to medical school, to pursue my music ministry. After graduating from college, I went to Miami to take a preparatory summer course, offered by a company called Stanley W. Kaplan.

When the preparatory course was finished, I returned to Chicago. Shortly before the date of the exam, I got a call from two dear friends, Joe and Mary Green. Joe managed a Christian bookstore in Brookfield, Illinois, and Mary worked with him. I had gotten to know them through my music. Their phone call brought tragic news. Their daughter, Patty, had died suddenly. They were in terrible agony, clinging desperately to their faith and trust in the Lord to see them through this difficult time.

"Jaime," they pleaded, "it would mean so much to us if you could play your violin at the memorial service." The funeral was going to be in Oklahoma, and I realized that it would take place a couple of days before the MCAT was scheduled. I had intended to do nothing but study and rest until the time of the exam. However, the Lord impressed me that I needed to be with Joe and Mary and do what little I could to help them.

"I'll be there," I assured my friends. A day later, I flew from Chicago to Oklahoma and participated in the memorial service. Afterwards, I returned to Chicago, and emotionally spent and physically exhausted, presented myself in the morning for the all-day exam. Today as I look back on that decision, I am so glad I followed the Lord's leading and chose to go to Joe and Mary's side when they needed me, The Lord blessed me back. When I got my MCAT exam results, they were very good indeed.

Even though I had done well on the MCAT, I would not know whether I was accepted to medical school for several more months. In the meantime, I decided to do another recording project. This time, I wanted to do something different from all the previous albums. The plan was to go to Europe, and record with the Czechoslovakian National Radio Symphony Orchestra. Although I could not afford to hire the entire orchestra, we could use a scaled-down group of twenty or so musicians to accomplish our purpose. A European orchestra and studio would be less expensive than recording in America. Of course, I didn't have enough money to do this project. That had not stopped me before. My good friends Paul and Stephen Tucker agreed to work with me, for a fraction of the sum they were usually paid.

I went to work to raise the thousands of dollars this project would need. I had met Herb and Linda Hill several years before. Herb was an executive at Hinsdale Hospital, in a suburb of Chicago. Linda managed the Apple Valley Health Food Store in Westmont, another nearby suburb. She had hired me to play the violin at the store's grand opening, and later gave me a job working there after my classes at the university. They had become dear friends. I asked Herb and Linda for help, and they didn't let me down. Through a friend of theirs who was a bank president, I was able to get an unsecured loan. They also persuaded other friends to invest in the project. My old friend Johne Perlick pitched in, too.

Next I went to see Dr. Walt Thompson and his wife, Avonne. I have deep respect for the Thompsons. They are two of the most dedicated and faithful Christians I have ever known. He's a surgeon who decided many years ago to use his money for God's glory. He and his wife live on less than ten percent of their income, giving the rest to the Lord's work. They agreed to help with the project.

Finally, I asked my friend Dr. Edwin "Nebb" Nebblett and his wife, María, for help. These friends have a deep appreciation for the ministry of music. The Nebbletts have four beautiful children all of whom play instruments. They also agreed to help.

Even though my friends had been generous with their assistance, I was still in a huge financial hole on the project. However, I believed the Lord wanted it to go forward. In October of 1992, I drove to Dallas, where Paul Tucker now lived, and spent three weeks with him as he arranged all of the songs. Meanwhile, his brother Stephen worked on the orchestral arrangements in California. Their relationship was so close that one could work on the keyboard arrangements, and the other on the orchestral arrangements. By talking back and forth on the phone, they blended their work beautifully. In November of 1992, Paul and Stephen, Dan Pabón, and I flew to Vienna, Austria. We rented a car, drove to Slovakia, and there we recorded *At the Cross* with the orchestra.

This was my first elaborate recording project. We recorded wonderful music, including "The Old Rugged Cross" and the "Hallelujah Chorus." It was exciting to have that excellent orchestra playing beautiful hymns. We had a fantastic and exciting time making the recording.

Even when the recording part was completed, there was much more to do. We had to mix and master the project and prepare it for duplication. I had to submit all of the pertinent information for the album cover, get the photographs taken, and oversee the cover design. Then the mass duplication of the album took place.

Recording an album is an incredibly intense experience. There is always a letdown afterwards. I always feel it strongly—almost like a depression. This project was no different. As we were driving back from the studio one day, Paul commented that I looked pretty down.

I admitted that I felt sad. "You go so hard for so long, and make all this beautiful music, and then it's over," I said. "It's a confusing feeling."

Paul looked at my long face and chuckled. "You have 'post-mixing syndrome,'" he said.

By the end of January of 1993, the project was ready to market. That is what you have to do next after you make an album. You have to go out and sell it. Since I was taking the year off from school, I had more time to devote to my music ministry. I went on the road, giving concerts every weekend and promoting the new album. My itinerary expanded to include some overseas trips, and I played concerts in Germany and other parts of Europe.

During this period, I got a phone call from Dr. Pat Mutch. She reminded me that we had met in Phoenix, Arizona. Dr. Mutch was head of the Institute of Alcohol and Drug Dependency in Berrien Springs, Michigan. "I'm taking a group of young people to Russia to do a Youth-to-Youth program," she told me. "I'd like to invite you to be a part of the team and put on a concert for these Russian young people." Then she said something that really got my attention. "We have asked to have our meetings and the final concert in the Kremlin Congress Party Hall." I agreed to go.

We flew to Russia in February of 1993. I have never been so cold in my life. Not even that first winter in Wisconsin could compare with it. It was 60 degrees below zero! There was no heat where we were staying, and the hot water lasted for only a few minutes each day. I didn't shower all week long. Only on the day of the final big performance, did I finally manage to shower and shave. As we walked outside each morning, and that frigid air hit us, we felt naked, despite the layers of coats we were wearing. I remember walking to an outdoor market on Arbat Street, where crafts and artifacts are set out for sale. By the time I had walked the two- or three-block length of this market and back, my feet were so numb I couldn't walk any farther.

Still it was exciting to be in Russia as a part of this team of young people, even though not everybody welcomed us warmly. In fact, while we were participating in an interview at a Russian television station, we learned that Russian Mafia members had called the station threatening action against our antidrug and alcohol campaign.

I met Dan Clark on that trip. Dan is a big guy. He was a football star in college. The Los Angeles Raiders drafted him, and he played linebacker for them for several years, until he suffered a career-ending injury that left him with a paralyzed left arm. However, this man was all dynamite. He fired up everybody in our group to use their talents for God's glory. He inspired us with his personal story. He told us how, after his accident, he was unable to move his arm. Every day he locked himself in a room alone and worked to make that arm move. At first he was able to move only a finger. He concentrated and worked for hours and hours more, and miraculously, today he enjoys nearly full motion in that arm. He and I worked together during that week in Russia. Now Dan is a motivational speaker who travels all over the world, sharing his positive message and his love for the Lord.

In the summer of 1993, Dan and I went to Latvia with Dr. Mutch's team, presenting an antidrug and alcohol program similar to the one we did in Russia. We had an opportunity while there to meet with the president of Latvia.

I believe Dan saved my life in Latvia. Every day we drove from our rooms in a suburb to the capital city of Riga. Our group traveled in a bus and a car. Usually the car was reserved for Dr. Mutch and Tom Neslund, who worked on projects such as this one in conjunction with the United Nations, but sometimes Dan and I rode in the car with them.

One day when the four of us were traveling together, we stopped at the house of a local church pastor to make a phone call. For some reason, I decided to stay in the car. Perhaps I wanted to keep an eye on our belongings—especially the violin—since the neighborhood was a little scary, but I really don't remember. Dan and the others were gone for quite a while, and I got anxious. Wondering what was keeping them, I got out of the car. Suddenly two men, one of whom had a knife, mugged me. I closed my eyes and prayed *Lord, help me!* The men were yelling at me, no doubt asking for my money or my watch. I yelled back. Of course, they were yelling in Latvian, and I was yelling in English. Realizing that they couldn't understand me, I yelled for Dan. "Dan!" I screamed. "Can you come out and help me?"

Fortunately, Dan heard. He came out of the house like a shot and saw what was going on. Thinking quickly, he picked up a log that was lying on the ground—and came running at us, shouting "Leave my friend alone!" The two men ran away in fear. Once again, the Lord had shown His mighty hand and delivered me from danger.

CHAPTER NINE

Medical School at Last

By June of 1993, I had heard from many of the dozen or so medical schools I had applied to. Most of them had turned me down. There were a couple of places I hadn't yet heard from yet, however, so hope was alive, and every phone call or letter I received was a possibility.

I was in Albuquerque, New Mexico, when my pager went off one afternoon. I didn't recognize the number, so my heart did a leap as I dialed it.

"Hello, this is Jaime Jorge," I said. From the other end of the line came a deep voice. "This is Dr. Jorge Girotti. I am the assistant dean at the University of Illinois Medical School. I wanted to let you know that we have accepted you into the Medical School at the Champaign-Urbana Campus. Your name is next on the list. I need to know if you intend to come."

I had been hoping the Chicago Campus would accept me so I could live at home while I attended medical school. Champaign-

Urbana was more than two hours south of the city. But I told him Yes on the spot, anyway. That was one of the happiest days of my life. I saw it as the fruition of my personal vision and dedication, and all the hard work of college. I had been preparing myself for this day for many years. Finally, the day had come, and I was to start medical school in less than three months. I had many other commitments, and it would take considerable effort to clear the deck and get ready, but I was excited. I thanked the Lord and happily shared the news with my friends and family.

Then I began to think more carefully about the decision I had just made. I had already booked concerts through the end of the year. I had again managed to pile on more debt, due to the last album I had made. I talked it over with my best advisors, Mima and Pipo. We agreed that if the University of Illinois would allow it, it would be better to defer my entrance into medical school for a year. I submitted my request to the university, and, thankfully, they agreed to allow me to wait until the fall of 1994 to start medical school.

Now that my goal was in sight, I redoubled my efforts to work as hard as I could to pay off all my debt. I wanted to walk into medical school without any financial worries. I also thought it would be a good thing to spend these final few months getting music and performing out of my system. I had never wanted to do it for a living—but I had to admit that I was enjoying the concertizing and the traveling. I loved meeting people and making friends all over the world. I took on even more concert dates. Working at music this hard would get it out of my system for sure. Then, when I started medical school, I would be able to concentrate, to serve one master.

In the fall of that year, I reestablished a relationship with a girl I had previously dated. We were not suited for each other, and I knew it. Even though I had asked for the Lord's help in the area of my relationships with the opposite sex, this time I failed to let the Lord lead, and the results were disastrous.

I have thought long and hard about how much of this part of my story I should reveal to my readers. I want to be honest and open with you. There isn't much point in telling your story if you leave some of it out, is there? So here goes. I'm going to call her Janet, although that's not her name.

I remember the night that she called. It was early October 1993. But first let me go back to four weeks before that. I had seen Janet when I performed a concert in the area where she lived. She heard that I was coming, and called to ask if we could get together. I said Yes, and we did. We talked about where we were in our lives. She said she still had feelings for me and asked if I felt the same way. I replied honestly that I no longer shared those feelings. In the year and a half since we had ended our relationship, I had moved on.

I could see that my words hurt her deeply. Having experienced a broken heart myself, I knew well the pain associated with rejection. As the evening ended, she asked if we could get together the next night, and I reluctantly said Yes, even though I knew that I should put an end to this relationship. I was aware that I should not put myself in temptation's way, but I agreed nonetheless.

The next evening Janet and I talked for several hours. Time passed quickly. It grew late, and I rose to leave. However, before I left, she asked me to "make love" to her. She said she had accepted the fact that I no longer had feelings for her. There were no strings attached, she assured me, and it would be a final goodbye. By then I had let things go too far, and didn't have the strength to say No. The entire time I felt guilty, but not for the right reasons. I remember telling her I felt there would be severe consequences for what we had done.

Four weeks went by. Then Janet called me. As soon as I heard her voice, I knew something was wrong. At first she fumbled over her words, saying that she was very sorry, that she didn't know how to tell me this. I asked her directly, "Are you pregnant?" There was quiet on the other end of the line for a few seconds. "Yes" she finally said.

After the first shock, I asked her some questions. She had not yet told her parents. She had not even confirmed that she was pregnant, but she was pretty sure. She asked me if perhaps we could get married and I told her No, I would not marry her.

We got off the phone without making any plans. I was scared to death. I didn't know what to do. I dreaded telling my family. I called my close friend Salim and blurted out the whole story. "Settle down and try to think about this calmly," he said. "You don't know this young lady very well. Can you be sure this is your child?" His question took me by surprise. The guilt of what I had done and the fear of the consequences had so overcome me that I hadn't even considered the possibility that the child might not be mine.

I went to my mother and confessed everything. Her shock and disappointment in me were devastating, but both her love for me and her faith in God remained steadfast. "Jaime," she said, "whatever happens, we're going to get through this, with God's help." I appreciated her reassurance, but I felt too guilty to turn to God for guidance and direction. Instead, I ran scared. I spent several sleepless nights, waiting for the official test results. I hoped against all hope that this was not true, but that was not to be. What would happen to me? What would people say or do? Would my church ostracize me? Would I be forsaken and never allowed to play the violin in a church again?

My family felt strongly that I should marry Janet, and wedding plans were quickly laid. As I contemplated marrying a girl I didn't love, I sank further into despair. I felt frustrated, alone, isolated, cut off from God. I considered suicide. Only the love and prayers of my family and friends prevented me from continuing down that path to self-destruction.

Finally, in my despair, I began to pray and earnestly seek the Lord, and there I found comfort. For the first time, I felt the Holy Spirit convicting me of the sin I had committed, and I humbly asked for forgiveness. I also asked the Lord to help me know whether marrying Janet was the right thing to do. After much prayer, thought, and advice from people who cared about me and were spiritually discerning, I concluded that it would be a great mistake to marry Janet.

And there was something else that was bothering me. As I thought back to the evening we had been together, I knew that I had taken precautions. A pregnancy seemed an almost impossible outcome. I realized that to ask her for proof that the baby was mine might seem a heartless thing to do, but I felt that I had a right to know. I asked Janet if she would have a blood test done. I told her that if the test proved the child was mine, I'd take full responsibility for him or her.

Her answer was puzzling. She told me she would not give me a blood test unless I married her first. The last time I had contact with her and her family, her mother said, "You need to decide what you're going to do, because if you don't marry her, she'll never give you a blood test, and she'll never let you see the baby."

To this day, I have never seen Janet again or her child. I still do not know if I am the child's father. I have chosen not to pursue a legal battle to obtain proof, for several reasons. I have prayed through the years for the well-being of this child and the mother and left the matter with the Lord, knowing that when the time is right, I will know, one way or another.

Despite the painful nature of this chapter in my life, I wanted to share it with you. This situation forced me, finally, to evaluate my life and my faith, and to renew my commitment to the Lord. That's the principal reason why I've included it in this book. With God's help, I finally made some changes. That is the good thing that came out of all this.

My hope and prayer is that every young person that reads this part of my story will learn from my mistake and realize that there is a proper time for everything. We honor God when we wait until marriage to enjoy what He created. We can do permanent and irreparable harm to ourselves and others when we do not follow His guidelines and the counsel found in the Bible.

In September of 1994, I started medical school. Things did not work out the way I had anticipated, however. It was like college all over again, only worse. I still had a load of debt. I was still looking for places to play to earn money, and I was still concertizing—in part to pay the bills—and frankly, because I enjoyed touching people with my music, and reaching them for the Lord.

At the end of the first semester, going into finals, I was failing almost every class. I was under a lot of stress again. and began to develop hives. Every evening around eight o'clock or so, I would start feeling strange. Then I would start itching, and within thirty minutes, big thick hives would appear all over my body.

At first, I thought it was an allergy, so I went to the doctor. "Well," he said, scratching his head. "This may be a temporary situation, or it may be a permanent one." That didn't help me much. He prescribed something called a "Prednisone-pack," which was a controlled dosage of Prednisone—starting with massive amounts, and tapering off a little more each day. I didn't want to take Prednisone after my earlier experience with its side effects, but I was desperate. I began to take the Prednisone-pack, and it worked. When I stopped taking it, the hives came back.

Despite all these problems, I was determined to make another album. I took my final exams at the beginning of December, and tried to put medical school out of my mind during the semester break. I had committed myself to the biggest recording project I had attempted thus far. We were going to record this album in the city of Bratislava, in what is now the country of Slovakia.

We planned to leave for Europe on Christmas day, 1994. We were all busy right up to the moment of departure, and had coordinated our schedules very tightly. I was flying from Chicago with my friend Salim Burgos, who was going to serve as production assistant for the project. I was delighted to have Salim help out on this project. We had known each other since eighth grade at North Shore Junior Academy, and had spent countless hours doing things together through the years. The Tucker twins, my arrangers/producers, were coming—Paul from Dallas and Stephen from Los Angeles. They planned to meet us in Chicago and fly with us to Europe. The orchestra was booked, awaiting our arrival.

On Christmas morning, I talked with Paul and Stephen, and all was well. Salim and I were finishing our packing before heading to O'Hare Airport when I got a page. It was from Stephen. I looked at my watch. *We're in big trouble,* I thought. *Stephen is supposed to be in the air right now.* I got to a phone as quickly as possible and called him on his cellular phone.

"I have very bad news," he reported. "They didn't let me get on the flight."

"What do you mean?" I asked, and he told me the sad story. He was bringing our digital recording equipment with him as checked luggage. Apparently, these cases were oversize and overweight, and the airlines had refused to accept them. People who fly frequently know that if you pay an excess baggage fee, you can get an oversize bag on a plane, but Stephen didn't know this. He had arrived late for his flight, and the counter agent had taken one look at his bags and told him he couldn't get his luggage on the plane.

I called Paul in Dallas immediately and said, "Look, Stephen missed his flight. Don't get on your plane now. Stay put until I call you back." Salim and I drove to the airport and spent three hours talking with the agents at American Airlines, explaining the situation. Our schedule involved flying to Frankfurt, and renting a vehicle for the ten-hour drive to Bratislava. We were planning to drive all day in order to arrive there late Monday night, so that we could begin recording on Tuesday morning.

"If we don't leave tonight," I explained to Cheryl Magnuson, the counter agent, "we can't possibly get there in time." She went to work immediately to get us on a later flight, a different plane, or a different airline. Nothing worked. We were feeling desperate.

Salim and I prayed. "Lord, this is Your project. This is Your money, Your work. Please help us somehow." Then we called Stephen and Paul again.

Stephen had been working on possible solutions to our problem. "The only thing I can think of is that we try to call our contact, Pavel Farkas," he said. Pavel was the concertmaster of the orchestra we had worked with on our previous European project, and was already in Europe making sure everything would be ready for our arrival.

Stephen called Pavel at his hotel. "We have a problem," he said, and explained that we were not going to be able to fly as scheduled. "Do you think it would be possible to contact all the musicians and change the recording start date from Tuesday to Wednesday?"

"Stephen, I'm sorry." Pavel replied, "I think that would be next to impossible. The players are coming from all over Europe. They are traveling here even as we speak, returning from their vacations. They're going to show up for recording on Tuesday."

Hanging up the phone, we considered our remaining options. If the musicians showed up on Tuesday, we were going to have to pay them, whether we were there or not. We needed three days of recording, and there was no way to know if we could extend our recording time by a day. There might be another project scheduled in the studio. Meanwhile, our friends at American Airlines were working furiously to help us get on another plane.

We called Pavel back. "Pavel, we know you said it's next to impossible, but would you try to contact some of the musicians?" we begged. He agreed, and we sat down to wait. After a couple of very long hours, he called us back.

"I really don't know how this is possible," Pavel told us, "but with the help of the orchestra manager, we were able to contact just about every single one of the sixty or seventy musicians. Not only did we reschedule each player, but we also rescheduled the recording session. Fortunately no other sessions were scheduled following ours, so we were able to change the recording time without any penalties."

We all breathed a huge sigh of relief. With the help of Cheryl from American Airlines, we were able to re-book on the same flight, one day later. We also solved the problem of the oversized luggage. Stephen got on his plane. He and Paul met us in Chicago, and the four of us flew together to Frankfurt one day later than scheduled. We arrived in Frankfurt early in the morning, after a sleepless night on the plane. We rented our vehicle, packed our gear, and began the long journey to Bratislava, arriving around midnight.

Early the next morning, bleary-eyed and exhausted, we arrived at the recording session. For our previous album, we had used fewer musicians, but this time we were recording with a full orchestra in a larger studio—a huge room that also served as an auditorium for live concerts.

But our problems weren't over. Our digital equipment cables didn't match the studio's inputs and plugs. We worked frantically to solve the problem. The orchestra sat patiently, knowing that, beginning at 8:00 A.M., they would get paid whether they played or not. The local engineers pitched in and helped us hand-make cables to plug into their main console and from there into our digital machines.

This worked after a fashion, but because we were unable to patch things together properly, we couldn't hear any of the music that was being recorded. When you're recording something, it's essential that you be able to hear what you're getting, so that you can correct any problems or distortions right away. We didn't have that luxury. All we could do was to look at the lights indicating whether each channel was recording. We decided to go ahead with recording the orchestra anyway, realizing that we wouldn't know if we had a useable recording until we got back to the United States.

I broke out in hives again. Stress, lack of sleep, and frustration overwhelmed me. As the engineers worked furiously to get the equipment to work, Stephen began to rehearse the orchestra. As I was running up stairs and down, between the studio and the control room, trying to help out wherever I could—and probably getting in the way—I heard the first strains of "How Great Thou Art" coming from the full orchestra. I sat down on the stairs and just cried. A sense of peace came over me. The music was so beautiful, so heavenly, and I was reminded of the reason we were doing all of this. *Lord Jesus,* I prayed. *Thank You for this tremendous opportunity. I ask that You bless this recording, and that You help us to get this done for Your honor and Your glory.* At that moment, my hives began to go away. They have never come back, to this day.

We finished three full days of recording on schedule, with still

Photo taken in 1994 for my new album

no way to hear any of the music we had recorded. Salim and I, who were sharing a room, were able to get some sleep that night. I do not know how Stephen and Paul managed. They spent many hours after each recording session preparing for the next day, making changes to the scores as needed. I don't know how they had the strength to do it, but they did.

Finally, on Saturday afternoon, December 31, 1994, we flew back to Chicago's O'Hare Airport together, with Stephen and Paul flying on to their respective cities from there. Four days later, I flew to Dallas to record the violin and finish the project. We still had drums, guitars, bass, saxophone, background vocals, and choirs to record. I spent four days in Dallas during the following week, recording the violin. On the weekend, while I was giving concerts, the other musicians came in and recorded their parts. We worked all day and sometimes all night, finishing around 2:00 A.M. We had to. We were running out of time and money.

After that marathon week, we moved the operation to Los Angeles for the final mixing of the album. Mixing a song can typically take a full day. We mixed thirteen songs in four days! We worked ourselves nearly to death, but by the grace of God, we finished the project on schedule. I wrote the checks for the bills, not knowing where the money was coming from. I trusted the Lord to provide and find a way. He always has and He always will. Somehow, I knew He would do it again.

CHAPTER TEN

Romance on the Basketball Court

In mid-January, after the Christmas break, I returned to medical school. I had no idea how I had done on my exams. I knew that I had been failing most of my classes before taking my finals. When I arrived back on campus, I went straight to the assistant dean's office to pick up my grades. As I left that office, I found a chair. I needed to sit down before I opened the envelope. I was nervous, anxious, worried, distraught, and depressed. I simply had no idea how I had done. When I opened the envelope, I nearly dropped the paper inside. I was shocked! I had done so well on every single test that I had pulled all of my grades up to above passing. OK, I know. Cramming had worked for me again. But I was truly astonished and grateful at the results. I believed it was a miracle.

Now I was back into the old grind that I had created for myself. School during the week and concerts on the weekend. I was still doing the final changes on the album, pushing hard so that I could release it and start to earn some money from it to pay back the costs. I needed to push. I had recorded this project on borrowed money, and it had gone $20,000 over budget. This debt was an overwhelming burden to a twenty-four-year-old kid in medical school, and I didn't know what I was going to do. I had charged most of those excess expenditures to my credit card. Its incredibly high interest rates were increasing the size of that debt every day, and I didn't know how I was going to pay any of it back.

Time was flying by, with all of the usual busyness of my life. Suddenly it was the first week in March, and I was in the middle of midterm exams. I had concerts that weekend in Arkansas. I had never been to Arkansas before. I kept a list of states I had performed in, and was looking forward to adding Arkansas to it.

Each time I went to a new place, I had developed the habit of thinking to myself, *Is this the trip where I'll meet the woman I'm going to marry?* As that thought crossed my mind this time, I remember wondering, *Am I too old?* Maybe it sounds silly to think that at twenty-four I thought I might be too old to get married, but my life was so hectic with school, concerts, and recording that I had very little time for a social life. In addition, I was still picking up the pieces from a bad relationship. I had put finding the right person on the back burner.

As I boarded the plane that Friday afternoon, right after finishing my midterms, again that old thought, *Is this the trip?* came into my mind. *Surely not,* I chided myself. *I'm not going to find anybody in Arkansas, of all places.* I settled down in my American Eagle airline seat and flew to Nashville, Tennessee, where I caught my connecting flight to Fayetteville, Arkansas.

I usually performed my weekend concerts in churches, and I often stayed with church members, or the pastor. This time, the pastor picked me up at the airport. The concert was taking place on Saturday night, and there was a performance at a nearby Christian school, Ozark Academy. I loved performing for the students, and had a wonderful weekend with opportunities to play often. Almost every concert is a wonderful experience for me, but there is one, every now and then, where there is a spirit, an electricity in the air, a connection with the audience that makes it special. That concert in Gentry, Arkansas, was one of those.

After the concert was over, I went out to the foyer of the church. There was a table set up there with my tapes and CDs for sale. As I usually do, I signed autographs and talked to people. After most of the people had left, a young lady came up to the table. She was tall, with long, caramel-colored hair. She wore a dark skirt and blouse, and high black leather boots. I was stunned. My first impression was "What a beautiful girl this is!"

Emily's note: Funny how the Lord works things out. I was in nursing school near Chattanooga, Tennessee, and I had decided at the very last minute to go home to Arkansas for spring break. I told myself I deserved a quiet weekend after my many hours of study. Gentry is a beautiful place, and my best friend Julie and I had planned to go for a long walk in the country. Julie suggested we go to a violin concert instead. When I objected, she promised me that if the musician wasn't very good, we would leave and go for our hike. Jaime was introduced that evening as a "highly eligible bachelor." I nudged Julie. "There's a guy for you," I said.

Now, I have to admit that being a "small-time celebrity" sometimes has had its rewards. Many times after a performance, I got the feeling that girls were eager to meet me. Not this one. She was reserved. She purchased a tape but didn't ask me to autograph it for her. I wanted to get to know her better, so I volunteered to autograph it and asked for her name. As I signed her cassette, she said, "I want you to know something. I came tonight with my friend, Julie," she said, and indicated another young lady, standing beside her. "We hadn't planned to stay for the entire concert. We thought we would come and listen for a bit and then go do some other things. But we enjoyed the concert so much that we stayed for the whole thing!"

I looked up into a pair of beautiful hazel eyes and said, "Well, I'm glad to hear that. I'm glad you enjoyed it. Thank you for staying, Emily."

"Well, it was nice to meet you," she said after we had talked for a few seconds more. "I've got to go."

Now I'm not a guy who is usually at a loss for words. But I didn't want this girl to get away, and I couldn't think of a thing to say to keep her.

"Wh-wh-where are you going?" I asked her. The question sounded silly to my own ears. I was embarrassed, but determined not to lose this opportunity. I didn't want this to be the last time that I ever saw this girl.

"We're just going down to the gym to play some basketball," she replied.

"Basketball? You play basketball? I love basketball!"

She smiled skeptically. "Really?" she asked.

"Yeah," I replied, feeling a big goofy grin spread across my face. "Do you think I could come along and play some basketball with you and your friend?"

"Well, OK," was her reply.

By this time, nearly everybody was gone. I gathered my things together very quickly. I found my violin and my accompaniment tracks and all my other stuff, and followed her out of the church foyer. She drove me back to the house where I was staying, and I quickly changed into a pair of shorts. I didn't have any basketball shoes, so we went back to her house, and she lent me a pair of her sneakers. I have rather small feet for a guy, so her shoes were wearable, if a little snug. Emily changed into blue shorts and a white top. She looked good enough to eat.

Then, we went to the gym, and even though I was exhausted from the concert, we played some fast basketball. The three of us had a great time. She and her friend Julie played against me and beat me. It was embarrassing. They were good.

Emily's note: Little did Jaime know that I had been voted Most Valuable Player on my college team and Julie was Athlete of the Year!

I was guarding Emily. Thinking I might distract her from her game and hoping to flirt with her a little, I said, "Nice legs."

"I don't get romantic on the basketball court," she shot right back. Then she dribbled right around me and laid up the ball for an easy basket.

All too soon, the basketball game ended.

Emily's note: As we were leaving the gym, Julie whispered to me, "Did you see the way that guy was looking at you?" "Nah," I replied. "He wasn't looking at me any special way."

As Emily was driving me back to the house where I was staying that night, I said, "Um, don't take this the wrong way, but I was wondering if we could be friends. Could I have your phone number?"

She seemed to be thinking it over. Then she said, "Well, I don't see why not," in an offhand, noncommittal sort of way. When we arrived at the pastor's house, she wrote her number down on a scrap of paper and gave it to me. I tucked it into my pocket, planning to guard it with my life!

I was so smitten. I had a terrible time getting to sleep that night. Was this love at first sight? It sure felt like it to me. But how did she feel about me? She was so cool and detached—I couldn't figure out whether she had liked me or not.

I had a performance early Sunday morning, and then the pastor who was my host planned to take me to the airport. I wanted to talk to Emily before I left. I dialed the number she had given me. I didn't have a clue what to say.

"Hello?"

"Could I please speak with Emily?" I asked, my voice croaking like a twelve-year-old's.

"This is Emily speaking," she replied. Her voice was soft and sweet.

"Hi, Emily, this is Jaime!" I said.

"Jaime who?" was the cool response.

"You know," I said desperately. "The guy who played the violin. The guy you played basketball with last night."

"Oh, yeah, right." she replied.

"Listen," I said. "I'm getting ready to leave for the airport and I wanted to say goodbye."

"Well, goodbye," she replied.

She's not going to make this easy, I thought. "Um, I know you just got home for spring break, and that you have a long drive back to Chattanooga next weekend," I said. She had told me this the night before, and that she was in nursing school at Southern College in Tennessee. She was going to be a nurse. I was going to be a doctor. That seemed pretty cool.

"So I know you have that long drive back to Chattanooga," I repeated lamely. "And I was wondering if you would call me when you get back to Tennessee, just to let me know that you're OK. So I won't worry."

"OK," she said. "I'll give you a call."

I gave her my phone number. It was going to be a long, long week. This was only Sunday. I lived all week long in anticipation of that phone call. The days dragged by. It was pure torture. Repeatedly I nearly picked up the phone. But I didn't want to call her. She had been rather brief and crisp with me. I needed to see if she was going to call me back.

The next weekend I flew to Washington State to do some concerts and perform on a radio program. It was my spring break weekend, so I was able to stay through Sunday night and fly home on Monday. Emily didn't know I was going to be away that weekend. I had given her only my home phone number, so I dialed my home answering machine every five minutes or so to see if she had called. No luck. That evening, I checked my answering machine again. Hallelujah! Emily had called! Her message was brief. "Hi, Jaime, it's Emily. I just wanted to let you know that I got home safely and thank you very much for the package.

"OK, well, I'll talk to you later. Goodbye."

Emily's note: Jaime sent me all of his CDs. Like any dorm student, I loved to get packages. I listened to them all and shared them with my friends.

Oh, that was an exciting day for me. What I heard in that simple message was that I could have hope. I called her back from Washington State, and we chatted. When I got home, I called her again, and wrote her a letter. She called me, and wrote back to me, and we began to communicate by phone and mail on a regular basis.

Something very important happened that weekend that briefly distracted me from thinking of Emily. You'll remember that I had maxed out my credit card to the tune of $20,000 paying the overbudget expenses on my latest recording project. January's bill came and I wasn't able to pay it. February's came, and I still didn't have the $20,000. Now March's bill was due, and I was coming up on ninety days overdue on my credit card. I needed to maintain good credit. I had no idea how I was ever going to pay this money. I was worried about it.

After I had performed for the church service, a man came up to me quietly and said, "Are you going to be at the fellowship luncheon?"

"Yes," I replied.

"Good," he said. "I'd like to talk to you."

"OK," I said. I didn't know what this was all about, but you meet all kinds of people when you concertize, so I'm used to such encounters. During lunch we talked further, and he told me he was a physician. "We have something in common," I replied, and told him about my being in medical school.

Usually I try to get in a little nap or a rest after lunch when I have several performances in one day, but after the fellowship luncheon was over, he came up to me again. "Would you be interested in taking a little time to go with me? I'd like to show you our office."

"Sure," I responded.

He showed me his wonderful medical facility, and we talked some more. I was impressed with his humility. He seemed like a dedicated Christian man. We relaxed in his office, and began to talk about all kinds of things. He opened up and told me about some of the exciting things as well as the challenges that he was facing. The things he shared were serious and confidential, and I was taken aback that he would share them with me, a person he had only just met.

When he stopped speaking, the only thing I could say was, "Doctor, would it be OK if we knelt down and prayed?" I didn't know what else to do.

We prayed together, and I said, "Lord, this is Your work and Your service. I ask that Your mighty hand be shown through all of our challenges and struggles, and that Your name be praised and honored."

Then he prayed, and as we rose from our knees, we hugged each other. Then, quite unexpectedly, he said, "I feel impressed to make a contribution to your ministry."

He took me off guard. I was not expecting this. He walked to his desk to get his checkbook. As he did, I sent up a silent prayer. *Lord, thank You for this kind man's generosity. You know that I need to make $1,500 every weekend from the album sales, the offering, and the honorariums to keep my music ministry going. If somehow You can impress this man to give me enough to make up that $1,500 this weekend, that would be wonderful.*

The doctor turned from his desk and held out a check to me. I was just going to take that check, put it in my pocket, and look at it later. I thought it wouldn't be polite to look at it immediately. But he made that impossible. He practically shoved the check in my face. I glanced at the number. The check was for $20,000. Not one penny less, not one penny more. In the weakness of my faith, I had asked for much less than I really needed. But God knew what my real need was.

I was overwhelmed. I threw myself at that man and hugged him hard. I thanked him and praised the Lord. Later that night, when I was alone, I wept for gratitude and joy. I couldn't believe what God had done for me that day. That debt, that horrible burden, was lifted. He had taken care of it. Praise the Lord! Here was another unequivocal sign from the Lord that, despite my faults and failures, He was with me, that He was not going to forsake me.

CHAPTER ELEVEN

Transition and Indecision

Even though I had seen Emily just one time so far, I was totally smitten by this lovely girl. She just turned me upside down. I had never felt like this about anybody before. It was a feeling so big that I hardly knew what to do with myself. I was so excited about Emily that I don't know how I managed to get through that semester of school. My grades were still a concern, my finances weren't completely resolved, (although the big debt was gone) and my concert schedule was just as heavy. But just thinking about Emily somehow helped me take on a brand new perspective. I was walking on clouds. I was studying and getting all my work done. I was completely happy.

I completed my second semester of my first year of medical school with no serious problems. No, that's not quite true. Something happened in late March of 1995. I had met Emily just four weeks prior to this. I was doing many weekend concerts. In some cases, I was cutting it pretty close—barely returning to school in time for exams, special classes, labs, and so forth. One weekend I flew to Palm

Springs, California, to perform at a special fund-raising weekend for a radio broadcast ministry called the Voice of Prophecy. I had met the director/speaker, Pastor Lonnie Melashenko, some time before and we had become friends.

I flew home on Sunday evening, arriving very late Sunday night. An anatomy skills exam was scheduled for 7:00 A.M. the next morning. This was the second to last exam of my first year of medical school. Well, guess what? I wasn't prepared. I hadn't done my homework, hadn't studied enough, and was in no way ready for this exam. I went straight to the lab from the plane, and spent all night there, cramming, but it was too little, too late. Still, I presented myself at the lab at 7:00 A.M. to take the test. This anatomy skills exam had twenty-four questions. You needed to get eighteen correct to pass. The test was given in the anatomy lab, where there were twelve stations with tagged cadavers at each station. You had to identify two tagged structures at each station. These structures could be muscles, veins, arteries, nerves, or bones. I flunked the test, horribly.

There was a rule that if you failed, but your score didn't fall below a certain level, you could retake the same exam several days later. If you didn't qualify for the special retake, you had only one more chance—another completely different exam would be given. This exam would decide your fate—a passing grade or total failure for the year. Well, I did so poorly that I didn't qualify for the retake. Three of my classmates were in the same boat. We waited for a date for the new exam to be posted. I still had six weeks of the semester left, with new material to learn every day. I had to learn all the old stuff I'd flunked out on, plus the new stuff so I wouldn't fall behind and have the same thing happen to me again next time around.

The new exam would take place in about a week and a half. On the assigned date, I arrived at the anatomy lab along with the three other students who had also failed the first time around. We put on our lab coats and gloves, picked up our writing pads and exam questions, and started working through the various stations, identifying the tagged structures on each cadaver. We had forty-five minutes to identify all twenty-four structures. The room was quiet. You could feel the concentration in the room, perhaps even the desperation.

When the forty-five minutes were up, Martha, the lab instructor, collected our papers. "When can we see the results?" we asked her.

The usual routine was that the test scores were put into the student mailboxes around 9:00 or 10:00 at night on the day of an exam. "You can pick them up tonight. They'll be in your boxes, as usual," Martha replied.

"Martha," we pleaded, "We can't wait that long! Can you please let us know sooner?"

The instructor took pity on us. "OK, wait outside," she said. "Since there are only four exams to grade, I'll do it now, and then I'll bring them out to you."

The four of us left the room. We took off our lab coats and washed our hands, trying vainly to rid ourselves of the stench of formaldehyde. Then we waited. And we waited some more. I couldn't stand the suspense, so I tip-toed back into the room where Martha was grading our papers, and stood behind her where she couldn't see me. I couldn't actually see the entire paper she was grading, but I could see enough to tell it wasn't mine. Neither was the second or the third one she graded. Finally she picked up my exam paper. Slowly and methodically she compared my answers with her answer sheet. Her right hand held a red pen. Unhurriedly she moved it down the page. If the hand stopped moving and jerked slightly, it meant that she was marking a wrong answer. I knew I could only get six wrong answers and still pass. Each answer was long and involved. I had prepared well for the exam this time, but in my nervousness, I knew I might have missed some little things. One little mistake, and the whole answer would be wrong. As I stood there, I saw her hand jerk slightly five times within the first ten answers. I realized that there were fourteen questions left, and that I could afford to get only one more wrong.

Please, Lord, I prayed through clenched teeth. *I can't afford to flunk out of my first year of medical school. Please help me pass this exam!* Slowly her hand slid down the remaining questions. It never jerked once.

Then I had to scramble quickly and slip back into the other room and act as if I didn't know what had happened. Martha gathered all the papers together, came into the room where we were waiting, and announced, "I have good news. You all passed the exam!"

As the second semester progressed, my friendship with Emily continued to grow through letters and phone calls, and we were eager to see each other again.

Emily's note: Actually, our phone bills rocketed. Sometimes Jaime would call me at three or four o'clock in the morning, and we would talk for hours. I fell in love with his voice.

The first free weekend I had, I invited her to come to Champaign-Urbana, where I was attending medical school, for a visit. At the time, I was living by myself in an apartment. Of course, I knew it would not be proper for the two of us to spend the weekend unchaperoned, so I asked my father to make the drive from Chicago to spend the weekend with us. He and Emily both arrived on Friday night.

Emily's note: I was nervous about seeing Jaime again. I redid my hair and changed my outfit several times. Jaime wasn't there to meet me when I arrived at the airport. First, I was irritated, then worried. Forty minutes later, as I was beginning to think about getting a flight back home, he showed up. He explained that he had hired a housekeeper to clean his apartment, and that he had had to drive her home. His big bear hug erased all my worry.

We had a wonderful time together. Emily was even more beautiful than I remembered. As lovely as she was on the outside, I was learning that she was even more beautiful inside, and that she had dedicated her heart to the Lord.

Like most young guys, I had a mental "wish-list" of attributes that I wanted my future wife to have. Somehow, when I met Emily, the list went out the window. I know it sounds sappy to say so, but she exceeded all my hopes and dreams. As I seriously considered my future, I realized that my list had changed. There were only three things on it now:

1. That she love God
2. That she love her family
3. That she love me

I figured that if any girl could meet those three requirements, the rest would take care of itself. I already knew that Emily loved the Lord first, and like me, she was very close to her family. Therefore, I knew she had her priorities right. Now it was up to me to persuade her to do the third thing on my list.

In May, I invited Emily to come to Chicago to meet the rest of the family. I pulled out all the stops to impress her, picking her up in a limousine, and taking her out to dinner at a fancy Italian restaurant called Cité, located in the penthouse of the Lake Point Tower on Chicago's Lake Shore Drive.

Emily's note: Jaime said to bring something formal to wear, but he wouldn't tell me why. Cité was the fanciest restaurant I had ever seen. It was circular, and there were more waiters than diners. Talk about a romantic place!

I even sang Emily a song, playing the restaurant's piano, much to the amusement of the staff. The owner's mother came by our table. "Darlin', you can play here anytime," she said. I was doing everything possible to woo Emily. I knew I was in love with her.

I began to sense that Emily could learn to love me too. We still hadn't said the words, but when the weekend was over, we agreed that we wanted to give our relationship an opportunity to grow.

Emily's note: It was the beginning of a magical relationship. We clicked. We complemented each other in so many ways. Jaime knew how to make me laugh. We could be in the middle of a serious conversation and he'd say something that would make me double over with laughter.

We decided that the next step was for Emily to move closer to where I lived so that we could spend more time getting to know each other. She had already completed a two-year nursing degree, so she was ready to make a change and start her nursing career. We decided that she would move to Champaign-Urbana near the medical school where I was living at the time. I flew down to Tennessee and helped her pack her things into her little car, and we drove together back to Champaign-Urbana.

Emily had saved up a little money. She soon found a nursing job at one of the town's two hospitals. Apartment hunting wasn't so easy, however. We needed to find something and get her settled quickly. At first, everything we looked at was too expensive or in a bad location or was too far from the hospital, or had something else wrong with it. Emily was getting stressed out and frustrated.

One morning I was sleeping late after a long night of catching up with work. Emily knocked on my door at what seemed like a ridiculously early hour, dressed and ready to do some more apartment hunting. When I opened to the door all sleepy-eyed and frazzled, she was upset.

"What am I going to do?" she cried. "I can't find an apartment. I've got to find a place to live, and you're sleeping!"

As you already know, I'm not at my best in the morning, and I was irritated with her for waking me up. "Look," I said, rather sharply. "You need to get down on your knees and pray. You need to ask the Lord to help you find an apartment." I turned on my heel, walked back into my bedroom and went to bed. I didn't hear another word from Emily. Of course, I didn't go back to sleep. I lay there, staring at the ceiling, hating myself for speaking to her in that harsh way, feeling guilty about using religion to get rid of her. I knew I needed to go after her, so I got out of bed, said a short prayer, and grabbed my clothes. As I came into the living room, there was Emily, on her knees, asking for Divine guidance and help. That day we found her a place to live, a little apartment not ten minutes away from mine.

The next few months were both exhilarating and difficult. Emily was working hard, but not making much money. She was barely able to pay her expenses and make ends meet. This was during my summer break from medical school, and I was touring like crazy, trying to use my time off to earn money to pay off my debts. We were both extremely busy, but we made as much time for each other as possible.

As my relationship with Emily grew more serious, I knew I had to tell her about my mistake with Janet. I wanted to be fair to Emily by telling her before she had committed herself too much to our relationship. In other words, I knew I needed to tell her early in our relationship, so that, once she knew all there was to know about me, she could choose whether she wanted me to remain in her life or not. Yet, I found it so very difficult to lay it all out for her.

When I finally told her the whole story, I felt as if someone had lifted a huge, suffocating burden off my back. I now had nothing to hide from the person with whom I wanted to spend the rest of my life.

Emily's note: Not long after Jaime told me about this part of his life, I left Illinois to finish my nursing degree in Tennessee. Our commitment became stronger as a result of the honest and open way Jaime and I dealt with it, and I returned to school feeling more confident than ever that Jaime and I were suited for each other, and that the Lord was in charge of this situation, as well as our relationship and our lives.

I knew without a doubt that Emily was the person the Lord wanted me to marry, and amazingly, she felt the same about me. We knew we were in love, and we were committed to making our relationship work, no matter what the odds. Even though we had some challenges with her work and my traveling, we had a wonderful time together in the summer and fall of 1995.

Emily's note: I had had a little taste of a lifestyle like Jaime's when I was just a kid. When I seven or eight, I sang in church quite a bit. This led to an opportunity to sing and travel with a child preacher—a boy about a year younger than I was. We traveled together for five years as an evangelistic team—he preached and I sang.

Fall came, and I began my second year of medical school. But somehow, this year, my heart wasn't in it like it had been before. During the summer I had had some wonderful experiences performing at arenas, camp meetings, churches, and other places. At a camp meeting in Washington State, a physician friend of mine came up to me after a concert and said, "You have been able to reach more people for God and touch their hearts here tonight then I have possibly reached in twenty years of medical practice."

That made me think. Was God trying to tell me something? Was I going to medical school for the right reasons? What did God want me to do? I was in a terrible quandary. I asked the medical school to give me some time off to consider my future, but was encouraged to continue my studies, even though I was unsure what my future would be. So I stayed in school. And I began to pray earnestly.

I thought about seeking advice from my friends and mentors, but it was difficult to admit to people that I was even thinking of leaving medical school. Besides, I had had enough advice already. Through the years, I had met many people who had encouraged me to make a music ministry my career choice. I had encountered just as many who advised me to become a physician. "Your musical talent is a unique gift, a real opportunity to reach out to people and influence them for good. God gave you that gift, and you need to use it for His glory," a friend whose opinion I respected would tell me, and I'd start to feel guilty about pursuing my goal of becoming a doctor.

"You can't leave medical school—you have to stick with it," another trusted friend would say. "You can still use your music to witness to others." That would make me feel bad about even considering giving up medical school.

It wasn't that I didn't have a mind of my own. But I had a difficult decision to make, and all this conflicting advice simply made it more difficult, so I decided not to tell anybody about my inner struggle—not my friends, not even my family. At first, I tried to keep it from Emily, too, but she could tell that something was wrong. So I told her what was on my heart, and thankfully, she accepted my struggle as her own. Together we continued to pray and ask God what He wanted us to do with our lives. Meanwhile, I continued in my second year at medical school.

CHAPTER TWELVE

The Way Becomes Clear

Toward the end of 1995, Emily and I decided that she should return to Tennessee and finish her four-year nursing degree. Our relationship had progressed to the point where we knew we were committed to each other. We hated to be apart, but we knew that it was important for her to finish her education.

I tried settling down to finish the second year of medical school, and to wrestle with the decision about my future. But I couldn't settle down. It was a tough time. Surely, I hadn't been dreaming all my life about wanting to be a doctor. I had always felt that the Lord was leading me in that direction. I had seen the powerful influence a godly physician can have, and I had felt called to a medical ministry all my life.

Yet the Lord was also opening doors that could lead to a wonderful future in music. On the other hand, a career in music ministry would mean a tough life. The performing, the concertizing, and the constant traveling were far from the glamorous lifestyle people imagined. I would be away from home for days and weeks at a time.

How would Emily deal with that? Could I make a living at it? What about the prestige connected with being a doctor? How important was that to me? Oh Lord, what should I do? At that point, I took a leave of absence from school to examine my future.

Emily and I talked for hours on the phone, weighing the pros and cons. She assured me that she supported me completely, whatever decision I made; as long as I was sure I was doing the Lord's will. That gave me a great deal of strength and comfort, but in the end, it was my decision. I was the one who had to make it.

I spent hours in prayer. I prayed and prayed. "Lord, please impress on me what I should do." But I wasn't being impressed, one way or the other. That was when I decided it was time to ask the Lord for a sign.

The school year had ended by this time. I prayed, "Lord, if it is Your will that I leave medical school to devote my life to full-time music ministry, I ask You to have someone call and tell me so." Since I had not told anybody that I was wrestling with this decision, I thought that would be a good test. I got up from my knees and looked at the phone. Nothing happened. I began to pace the floor. Still nothing happened. Ten minutes passed, and then the phone rang.

"Listen," a friend of mine said, "I have no idea what made me call you, but I feel impressed to tell you something." I held my breath as he continued. "I really think that what you should be doing is full-time music ministry," he said, "and not medicine."

I didn't know what to say. "Well, thanks," I said. "I appreciate your letting me know how you feel." I hung up the phone, fell into the nearest chair, and held my head in both hands. I couldn't believe what had happened. I had asked God for a sign. I expected a sign, but when it came, I wasn't sure it was for real. Doubt crept into my mind. Maybe that phone call was just a coincidence. I couldn't make this decision on the basis of a coincidence, could I? Leaving medical school was such a big step. I had to be sure. I was more scared and confused than ever.

I thought about the Bible story of Gideon. Gideon put out his fleece, and when the Lord gave him a sign, Gideon said, "Lord, please, could I have another sign?"

So I went back on my knees. "Oh Lord, I guess I need a second opinion, or something. If I'm going to leave medical school, I'm going to need to move out of this apartment. As far as I know, my lease was automatically renewed for another year at the end of May. I don't want to break my contract. If that lease wasn't renewed, I'll know You want me to leave medical school and devote my life to a music ministry."

Then I got in my car and drove to my apartment manager's office. I had signed an ironclad lease that was renewed automatically every May 31, unless I informed the management otherwise. Now it was nearly the end of June. The manager welcomed me into her office. "Hi, Jaime," she said. "Have a seat. We haven't seen you down here in a while. Is everything all right with the apartment?"

"Yes, ma'am," I replied. "But I need to talk to you about my lease. You know I came here to study medicine, and I've been here for two years. But there's a chance that my plans might change in the near future, and I might need to leave the apartment."

She looked at me quizzically. I tried to read her expression, but her face gave nothing away.

I continued, "I know that I should have let you know about this by the end of May, before my lease was automatically renewed for another year."

"Well, actually, that's not quite true," the manager responded.

My heart took a leap.

"We're experimenting with a grace period for the first time this year," she said.

"Well, when is the deadline?"

"It's been extended for thirty days. You need to let us know something by the end of June," she replied.

I looked at the calendar on my watch. It was June 29. I had my second sign. I took a deep breath and said, "Ma'am, I'm leaving medical school. I won't need to renew my lease."

"That's fine," she said with a smile, and handed me some papers to fill out.

As I drove home, my heart was overflowing. I had been sure I was locked into that lease. God was so amazing! I had made a decision. The burden was lifted. I felt deeply grateful for His leading. I knew what He wanted me to do, and that He would be with me every step of the way. "Step out in faith," He was saying to me. "Let me worry about your problems. I'll make sure you make a living. You go out and share your talent and your witness, and I'll do the rest."

Now that I had made the decision, I was filled with peace. The first thing I did was to tell my parents and Emily. I knew that I had Emily's complete support, but what would Mima and Pipo say? Even though Pipo had some hopes that I would enter the ministry, and Mima had dreamed of my having a musical career, they had always known that I intended to be a physician, and they had supported me every step of the way.

Mima answered the phone when I called. "Mima, I'm leaving medical school and going into a full-time music ministry," I blurted. There was silence on the other end of the line. I went on, "I've been struggling with this decision. I know you knew that I was struggling with something. I've been praying about it, and the Lord has made it clear to me that this is what He wants me to do."

Mima was so happy her words tumbled over each other. Laughter and tears mingled in her voice as she exclaimed, "I want you to know, Jaimito, that I've been very worried about you. I know how hard it's been these last few years—going to school, doing two or three concerts every weekend, taking exams when you were so tired! I am so relieved. Music is what you should be doing. The Lord gave you an incredible talent. I'm so excited for you!"

Pipo was happy too. Maybe there was going to be another minister in the family, after all—even if he did preach with a violin.

Next I sat down and wrote a letter to about a hundred of my closest friends—people who had supported me, and were praying for me. I wanted them to hear about my exciting new future from me, and to seek their prayers as I faced some drastic changes. Thank God that He created us all so that we would find comfort, strength, and help in one another.

CHAPTER THIRTEEN

Starting a Whole New Life

Now the big question was, "What am I going to do next?" I had no reason to stay in Champaign-Urbana, where the medical school was. Would I move back in with my parents in Chicago, or go somewhere else? I needed to do so many things. First, I needed a fantastic booking agent—someone who could get me the concerts I would need to make a music ministry pay the bills. I could live at home and save money while I tried to get a full-time ministry going—or I could go somewhere else. I also needed some way to support myself until I was able to do music full time.

Then another door opened up. Leonel had a practice in Shelby, North Carolina. He needed an administrator and office manager. I didn't know a thing about running a medical office, but in a sense I had been running my own business for a long time. He offered me the job. I gave it some serious thought. I would be able to live with Leonel, earn an income, and get my musical career going. It would give me a chance to witness to him, too—something I felt I had never done very well.

I talked with Mima and Pipo about it. They agreed that it was a good idea, and so, in September of 1996, just two and a half months after I made up my mind to leave medical school, I packed my bags and moved to Kings Mountain, North Carolina.

Leaving Illinois was scary and sad. Even though I had been living in my own apartment for some time, my parents weren't very far away. Our family was a small, tight-knit one. Six of us had come from Cuba; Mima, Pipo, May and me, my grandmother Bayba and Uncle Leonel. All of us but Leonel had been together since shortly after we left Cuba. Now, at twenty-five, I was finally leaving the nest. It was hard to say goodbye. We spent a couple of days together in Chicago before I left, laughing, talking, praying and crying together. Finally, the time came, and, with a loaded-down U-Haul trailer behind me, I set out on the long journey to North Carolina.

The medical practice was busy. I did a little bit of everything, from filing to secretarial work, to collections—often working twelve-hour days. About the time I arrived, my sister May, who had just finished her college classes, came to live with my uncle and me and work at the practice. The three of us rented a house together, and became a family. At the same time, I was also working diligently to set up concert bookings—still convinced God wanted me to go in this direction.

One of the first bookings I arranged was a weekend of concerts in northern Georgia at a beautiful Christian camp and resort called Cohutta Springs, located about an hour from Emily's nursing school in Tennessee. I had been searching for the right time and place to propose to her, and this upcoming weekend might be a good opportunity to pop the question. I had been to Cohutta Springs before. It was a beautiful, peaceful place. I asked her to join me there, but gave her no hint of what I had in mind. I wanted it to be a total surprise.

The week before, I did something I had watched several of my friends do. It had always intrigued me, and I had looked forward to doing it myself someday. Now it was my turn. I shopped for Emily's engagement present. I chose to get her a watch, rather than a ring. I shopped long and carefully, choosing exactly the right one. I had it gift-wrapped, and tucked it inside the jeweler's paper bag. On Friday afternoon, as I packed the car for the five-hour drive to the north Georgia resort, May spied the bag. Putting two and two together, and using her woman's intuition to make five or six, she asked, "Are you going to ask Emily to marry you?"

I was so surprised that she had figured out my plans that I blurted out my secret. "Yes!" May was excited and thrilled. She jumped up and down and hugged me hard, squealing, laughing, and crying all at the same time. Her reaction puzzled me, but I found out later, by watching Emily's friends, that they all did the same thing. When they heard the news they all jumped up and down, laughed, hugged, and cried, just like May. It is an interesting thing for a guy to watch.

It was the last weekend in September. I drove from Charlotte to Asheville, on to Knoxville and Chattanooga, so filled with excitement and anticipation that I barely noticed the beautiful scenery and early fall foliage.

As soon as my first presentation was over and we had some time to ourselves, I invited Emily to go for a walk along the camp's trails. The day was beautiful, and the scenery was breathtaking with a sparkling blue lake and tree-covered mountains. I brought my guitar with me, the watch concealed in the guitar case.

Emily's note: I remember thinking, It isn't like Jaime to bring his guitar on a walk, *but I knew how spontaneous he could be, so I dismissed it as a whim.*

We found a secluded spot on a rocky ridge, overlooking the lake and the lodge below. I took out my guitar and played and sang some old familiar hymns and campfire songs. Emily sang along in her lovely voice.

I knelt to put the guitar back in its case, and to take the watch out. As I turned back to look at Emily, she had just stood up. Now I was in the classic "pop the question" position. Taking her hand in mine, I looked into her eyes and said, "Emily, you know that I love you and want to spend my life with you. Will you marry me?"

Well, I took her by surprise, all right. She was so shocked that she thought I was joking. "Are you serious?" she asked.

"Yeah!" I said.

Emily's note: I laughed! We had kidded a little about getting married, so my first thought was that this was another of his jokes. Poor Jaime! He looked rather forlorn, there on his knees in the dirt.

Somehow, I made her understand that I was more serious than I had ever been in my life. She said Yes, and I gave her the watch. That night at the concert, I announced that Emily had agreed to be my wife. Then there was a lot more of that laughing, hugging, and jumping up and down.

I can't tell you how happy I was when Emily said Yes. Sometimes I had to pinch myself to make sure it was real. I suppose, when we are kids, we all think about getting married someday. We dream about the person we're going to meet and marry. I just praised the Lord because He had found somebody for me who was lovelier and sweeter than I could ever have imagined.

I told my family right away, and they were thrilled for us, as were my friends. We discussed a wedding date. Emily still needed two more semesters to complete her bachelor's degree in nursing, so it made good sense to wait until she graduated to get married. We began to make plans for the wedding. I had some ideas, particularly about the music, but all the rest of it was a girl thing, and I left it to Emily. All I know is that it was a long, long wait from September 26, 1996 to our wedding day on August 31, 1997.

The wedding plans began to take shape. Emily and I both wanted it to be a time when we could enjoy the company of our family and dearest friends. I was in charge of the music. We had decided to have a twenty-piece string ensemble. Stephen and Paul Tucker agreed to select the music, and Stephen offered to compose an original bridal march for Emily. I had so many musician friends, and we wanted them all to be a part of the service. I thought of Judy Wolter-Bailey, the harpist, and the children of my good friends the Nebbletts, and my great friend Dr. Steve Peterson, who played the saxophone, and Del Delker, a special friend with a beautiful contralto voice. As soon as we set the date, I got in touch with these friends and many others, and told them that it would mean the world to Emily and me if they could attend our wedding. The wedding would be held in Emily's hometown, Gentry, Arkansas, in the church where we had met.

The time flew by, and soon our wedding day was only weeks away. The week before, I performed at Richey Street Baptist Church, in Pasadena, Texas, a place where I had been invited to perform several times. Emily surprised me by meeting me in Texas, and we flew together to Gentry, to spend the week before the wedding. A flurry of last-minute details filled that interesting and exhausting week. Guests arrived from all over the United States, and even the world. One of my groomsmen, Marko Dedic, arrived from Germany.

At the wedding rehearsal, the night before the big day, I had to leave the dinner and play for a Spanish group at a nearby church. I participated in the rehearsal and the first part of the dinner, slipped away to perform, and came back to the dinner. We had a great time with family and friends, and I got to bed very late. I was just getting to sleep when the groomsmen, all supposedly good friends of mine, burst into my room, dragged me out of bed, and dumped me into the swimming pool. After more prewedding shenanigans, during which somehow part of my legs got shaved, I was finally allowed to go to bed and get a little sleep.

Our wedding day dawned beautiful and bright. My heart was pounding as I arrived at the church. The music was everything we had hoped for. All of the friends I had asked to perform were there, even Del Delker all the way from California. The church was packed with people, but when the bridal march began and the doors at the back opened, it seemed that I stood there alone, waiting for my bride. When I saw my beautiful Emily come through those doors in her lovely white wedding gown, with a wreath of flowers in her hair, the world stood still. My knees turned to jelly. I was shaking and very near tears. It was the most incredible moment of my life.

The ceremony went beautifully. Lonnie Melashenko, my pastor friend from California, whom I'd gotten to know over the years, officiated. On his recommendation, we had done some premarital counseling with the wife of the pastor of the church I attended in

Fletcher, North Carolina. In one of our counseling sessions, she had suggested that we might want to write our own wedding vows. These were the words we said to each other:

Jaime's Vows: *It's hard for me to believe that this day has finally come. For years I've asked the Lord to send me the right one for me. He sent me someone better than I ever dreamed of. He sent you. This is the greatest day of my life. The only day that will surpass this one will be the day that I hear the words, "Well done, good and faithful servant . . ."*

Until that day arrives, I promise to do my best so that our new home will be a piece of heaven on earth. I promise to love you, protect you and care for you during the good and bad times, for better or worse, for richer or poorer, and I will honor you by keeping myself only for you. May you always see Christ in me and may Christ be the center of our happy home.

Emily's Vows: *I am so honored to be standing up here with you as your wife-to-be, friend, and most importantly, Christian companion. Through your love for God and your example, my relationship with Christ has been strengthened. I love you, Jaime, not only for what you are, but for what I am when I'm with you.*

Words cannot express the joy I have when we're together. You will always be the miracle that makes my life complete. I pray I will be like the wife described in Proverbs 31: "Who can find a wife of noble character? She is worth more than the costliest of jewels. Her husband has total confidence in her. He will never be poor. She is respected and she's not afraid of the future. She speaks words of gentle wisdom and teaches kindness to others."

And if along the way we find it starts to storm, you have the assurance and promise of my love. Yes, I will love you, laugh with you, hold you, and honor you; respect, encourage, and cherish you, in health and in sickness, through sorrow and success for all the days of my life.

Our wedding day was truly a magical day for both of us. It was such a joy to be surrounded by dear friends. Some couldn't be there, of course, but we knew they were thinking of us. Our wedding party included Edwin Mastrapa, whose family had been friends with mine since we

Wedding day, August
31, 1997. One of the
greatest days of my life!

Dad and Mom Hall
(Estle and Delores),
Emily, me, Mima, and Pipo.

were kids together in Cuba, and Manny Pastor, whose dad had offered my dad a job in Chicago, and of course, Salim, my friend of many years, my partner in crime, and my adversary in basketball games.

Looking out over the audience, I saw many familiar faces. George and Zorisa Selak came from Chicago. George and I had played violin together in orchestras dozens of times. Uncle Henry and Aunt Hilda Niemann came from California. I had met them at a concert once, and ever since, whenever I traveled near their area, I had a home. Cheryl Magnuson was there—my faithful friend from American Airlines who has assisted me with travel. So many dear faces! The Hills, the Nebbletts, and the Petersons were there. The Mutchs, Dan and Betsy Matthews . . . I can't possibly name them all. Dan Clark, my old friend from trips to Moscow and Latvia, was the master of ceremonies at the reception. He and his entire family had come to the wedding all the way from Salt Lake City, Utah. Dan is quite a character, and the reception was a lot of fun.

We spent our honeymoon in Jamaica. It was a wonderful time of getting to know each other, even though I suffered some withdrawal pains, because we had no phones, no Internet, no pagers, little contact with the outside world. But it was just what we both needed, after the excitement and pressure of the wedding and our usual busy lives.

When we returned to Gentry, we crammed all of Emily's belongings into her little Toyota Tercel and made the fifteen-hour trip to North Carolina. As soon as we arrived, I took off for Guam to do some concerts and speaking engagements. This travel and separation would become an inevitable part of our marriage because it is a part of the ministry we have chosen, but it's something we've never been able to get used to.

Before the wedding, I had wondered what being married would be like. I had always been an independent person. I had lived in my own apartment for a couple of years. I have to admit I was a little apprehensive.

Emily and I had talked a lot about how we were going to live. We were determined that our marriage and the home we made together would be a lasting piece of heaven on earth. We wanted to spend as much time together as possible. We decided that, at least for the first few months, Emily would not go to work, even though she could have easily found a nursing job, so that she would be free to travel with me. We knew we would be poor during this time, because we had heavy debts and expenses, but we would be together, and that was more important than making money.

So, Emily went with me almost everywhere I went for the first three years of our marriage. I believe that people appreciated the presentations and the concerts even more, and that our witness as a committed couple was greater than anything I had been able to do alone.

Emily's note: I love to watch Jaime in action. He is an audience-based musician and speaker. He can be completely impromptu. He'll change his repertoire if the audience isn't responding. It's amazing to see people in the audience go from laughing to crying within an hour. He truly communicates with his audience. When I began to travel with Jaime I gained a whole new perspective on music ministry. I know God brought us together and I believe that my early experiences with traveling and singing have helped to prepare me for our life together.

It wasn't always possible for us to travel together. In 1998, for instance, I went to Brazil six times. Those tours were extremely long and exhausting, involving all-night flying to get there, followed by a grueling schedule of ten concerts in eight days—with more flying between concerts. Emily joined me once or twice, but after that, we agreed that she should stay home when I went to Brazil. This was painful for both of us. "Oh, honey, can you please come home?" she'd plead when I called her. "I miss you so much. I'm so lonely!" Today, as I travel all over the world, there are still times when we're apart for days at a time. This will always be difficult for both of us, but it gives us a deep appreciation for the time we spend together.

Emily's note: *I didn't understand what Jaime's life is like until I had traveled with him for at least a year. It is impossible to explain what life on the road is like—you have to experience it.*

Let me tell you something about one of the tours in Brazil. I've already mentioned that those tours were grueling. Brazil is a big country. We would travel all day—either flying or driving—give a concert, and then often, drive or fly all night to the next city. We gave concerts every night of the week, and often did two more per day on the weekends. We played in churches of all denominations—Baptist, Methodist, Presbyterian, and Seventh-day Adventist. There were three of us in our group. Ruimar Paiva, a Brazilian who was studying in the United States, was my translator. Olair Dos Santos was my contact person and agent. Olair is one of the funniest people I've ever known. His sense of humor took much of the tedium out of our travel. We called him "Barba," which is the Portuguese word for beard—for obvious reasons. Sometimes Barba's wife, Beatriz, a talented pianist, would join us. Then the two of us would give classical concerts in cultural centers, theaters, and auditoriums throughout Brazil.

One night we were scheduled to perform in Olair's and Beatriz's home town of Araçatuba, a city of 100,000 people. As we arrived in the city and drove through its streets, we realized that a large portion—if not all of the city—was completely dark. I began to worry. I knew that if we didn't have electricity, we'd have no CD player for accompaniment tracks, no microphones, and worst of all, no light! We would have to cancel the concert. Silently I said a prayer that God would help us find a way to bring our message to these people.

Slowly we made our way through the dark streets to the church where we were to perform. As we neared the part of town where the church was located, we noticed that many people were out walking on the streets. They seemed to be moving in the direction of the church. As we turned the corner, we saw something splendid. The church was lit up with glorious light—the only building in the whole neighborhood that had power. As it turned out, many of the people we saw walking toward the church weren't planning to go there that evening. They came because there was light in the church. The hand of God was over us once again, and we were given a wonderful opportunity for a spiritual object lesson. The church had the only power, the only light in the whole community that night.

CHAPTER FOURTEEN

The Christmas Project

During those many long nights of traveling in Brazil, I began to think seriously about a project I had always wanted to do. By 1998, I had recorded seven albums, with the Lord's help. The first six were all religious music, but the most recent one was a combination of classical and popular music. I had pondered the wisdom of doing a non-religious album for a long time before actually doing it. I didn't always perform in churches. Just as my audiences in churches responded to hymns they knew and loved, so my audiences in public halls appreciated familiar secular music. I often began those concerts with something classical and some old-fashioned popular songs, before moving into religious music and my personal witness for Jesus.

Now I wanted to add a Christmas album to this collection. Christmas is very special to me. Having been born in communist Cuba, I didn't even know very much about Christmas until my family and I came to the United States. In addition, I thought a Christmas album would be a good way to reach people with the gospel, since many people who don't go to church at any other time will come to a Christmas service or concert.

How to make it happen? A Christmas album must be timeless. People should be able to play it year after year without thinking it dated. It had to be done right. I well knew, from my previous experiences, that it would be expensive. In fact, it would no doubt be enormously expensive—the biggest project I had tackled thus far. I didn't have that kind of money.

I puzzled over this project during those long Brazilian nights as we drove through the empty countryside from one concert site to another. I prayed about it. "Lord, if You want this album to be done, please open the doors and make it possible." Sleepless nights followed as the dream took shape. I developed a budget, and the size of it nearly frightened me into forgetting the whole thing. Then, one night, as I lay awake in a Brazilian hotel room, running the figures over and over in my head, I had an idea. I knew how to raise the funds I would need. "Yes!" I shouted into the darkness. The Lord had given me the answer I needed.

The plan was simple. I had made many friends over the years, through my travels and concertizing. Because of my connection to medicine, many of these friends and acquaintances were a part of the medical profession, from physicians to health care administrators. I would go to these people and ask them to purchase my Christmas CD in advance, as a gift for their employees. I quickly put together a list. It was possible! If I could just get enough of these good friends to participate, I could raise enough money to do the project.

It was already autumn of 1998. I set to work lining up concerts for 1999, concentrating on areas of the country where there were people who might help with the Christmas album by pre-purchasing CDs for their employees. I also created a proposal for the project, to show people what they could expect.

My music ministry was growing. About this time, I stopped working at the medical practice to concentrate on my ministry full time. I had found a wonderful booking agent in Linda Hill, who had been my good friend for a number of years. She had never been a booking agent before, but she knew how to talk to people, and she had a real passion for my music ministry. Many times, she'd call churches or other organizations cold turkey. They'd turn her down initially, but she'd persist, and I'd get booked into places where there had previously been no interest.

Linda and her husband, Herb, had helped me raise money for previous albums, and she recommended some other avenues for me to explore for the Christmas album's funding. I eagerly followed up on them.

Emily and I were living in an apartment building that also housed the medical practice. In addition to traveling with me, Emily occasionally filled in as a nurse in the office, and picked up some part-time work in a nearby hospital. My parents and Bayba had recently moved to North Carolina, and were living about an hour away. I did not get to see my family often, however, because I was traveling so much. Emily went with me as much as she possibly could, but the pressures of traveling were getting her down. Emily has asthma, a condition she has suffered from her entire life. Traveling exhausted her and caused the asthma to flare up. Eventually, the time would come when she would have to stop most of her traveling with me, but in 1998, she was still trying to go here, there, and everywhere I went.

The year 1999 was definitely one for the books. During this year, our faith was tested in many ways. The Christmas project was the primary reason for this. For the first few months of the year, I maintained a full concert schedule while also knocking on a great many doors, soliciting support for the project. I was determined not to ask people to donate money. I wanted to earn the needed development funds by pre-selling the album.

I figured that the project would cost around $80,000. That may sound like a lot of money, but it is a pittance compared to what such projects usually cost. Recording an album like this in Hollywood or Nashville could easily have cost a million dollars or more. My $80,000 was a shoestring budget. The pre-selling was progressing, although some of the companies and organizations balked at paying the full amount up front. Some were unwilling to take a chance at all. "When you deliver the product," they told me, "we'll be happy to buy it."

Some money was coming in, however, and we began to spend it on the initial phases of the project. I knew I wanted to work with Paul and Stephen Tucker again. I was counting on their friendship and expertise for this important project. I contacted several European orchestras, including the Czecho-Slovak National Radio Symphony Orchestra we had used before. They weren't available. I talked to representatives from several other orchestras. Nothing worked out. Stephen Tucker had a friend, Susanna Darvasi, who was Hungarian, and through her, we contacted the Hungarian National Philharmonic Orchestra, based in Budapest. They were willing to do the project! Susanna agreed to go to Europe with us and be our translator.

The Lord has led me to so many people in my life who have turned out to be a special blessing. Sometimes I've helped them, but more often, they've helped me. In 1998, I met a man on a plane while returning from one of my trips to Brazil. We talked, as strangers sometimes do on long trips. He asked me what I did, and because it was uppermost in my mind at the time, I told him about the Christmas project. I learned that his name was John Blackburn. He was the president and general manager of a mountain resort near Linville, North Carolina, called Eseeola Lodge. He invited me to come and stay at his resort sometime. Later, I sent him a couple of CDs and we began a friendship.

When John learned that I was planning to spend several days strategizing with Paul and Stephen, he asked us to be his guests at Eseeola Lodge. The twins and another friend, Trent DeLong, joined Emily and me there for three days in early June of 1999. In this beautiful setting, we chose the music, determined the styles, and decided who was going to arrange what. As before, the brothers blended their talents into an unbeatable musical team. Stephen did the orchestral arranging, and Paul arranged for the keyboards and the choir. He would do the engineering as well. In three days, we had the final song list and knew exactly what musical direction the album would take. We all appreciated Mr. Blackburn's kind hospitality, and he followed that up by supporting the Christmas project financially, as if he hadn't already done enough.

I had invited Trent along to watch Paul and Stephen in action. He is a young vocalist who was thinking of starting a recording project, and I wanted him to see how they worked. I had rented a Ford Explorer to drive to Eseeola Lodge—our little Toyota Tercel was just too small for the five of us. Trent had driven up in the Tercel, and we agreed that he would drive the Tercel back to Charlotte Airport, since he had to leave earlier than the rest of us.

Several hours after he had left for the airport, I got a phone call from Trent's father. "I want you to know that everything's fine. Trent is OK, but he had an accident on the way to the airport. I'm afraid your car is totaled."

Well, we needed a new car anyway. The situation turned out all right. We were able to use the insurance money as a down payment on a Chevy Tahoe, a vehicle much better suited to all the traveling we were doing. I've kidded Trent many times since, "The next time we need a new car, I'm going to ask you to come over and drive the old one."

The night before Paul and Stephen were to leave, I noticed that Stephen had become unusually quiet and withdrawn. "What's wrong?" I asked.

"I'm just realizing how much work I'm going to have to do on this project," he said soberly. "I'd better start saving up my energy!"

That's how it was for all of us during the entire project. Work, work, work.

We flew to Hungary on Thursday, the 15th of July, arriving absolutely exhausted from the preparations and the overnight flight. The orchestra manager, László Samu, and his wife, Gabi, met us, accompanied by Susanna, our translator, who had come on ahead of us.

The Petersons, Steve, Bonnie, and Scott, met us at the motel. I had invited my close friend, Steve, and his family to observe the recording sessions as a part of their vacation.

While Emily and the rest of the group caught up on their sleep, I went with Susanna and László to make the first of the agreed-upon payments for the project. I had brought $15,000 with me in travelers' checks. I had already made an initial payment to Paul and Steven, as was customary, as well as made other payments related to the trip. Now I had to turn $12,000 over to László, paying for half of the costs of the recording session. I thought László would be happy to have travelers' checks.

"What are travelers' checks?" he asked, looking at them and shaking his head in a puzzled way. He didn't know what they were and didn't want them. He wanted cash.

"OK," I said. "No problem. I'll just go to the American Express office and exchange the travelers' checks for U.S. dollars. So I did. The only hitch was, American Express charged a hefty fee for this service, and I came up more than $1,000 poorer after this transaction. This was not good news—my money was dwindling fast.

We planned three full days of recording. That's not a lot of recording time, and we had much music to record. The orchestra sounded wonderful. I love the recording process. It's exciting, it's tense, and it's a roller coaster. Add to all that the tremendous joy of having Emily there this time, sharing it with me, and I was bursting with excitement.

The first two days of recording went well. The team worked smoothly together. It was fulfilling to share this experience with good friends. I appreciated getting to know Susanna, our translator. Her positive attitude and faith in the Lord inspired and encouraged all of us. That woman didn't know the meaning of the word "no."

By day three, the recording had gone so well that Stephen was racing to get the last of the arrangements written so that we could record them. Stephen was expecting the scores of two pieces to be emailed from the United States. We went to a little Internet café in Budapest to download the email. Stephen signed on, and we waited a very long time. Finally, one of the two pieces came through. Stephen gave up on the other score. He printed out what he had received and left the café. Susanna was waiting on the sidewalk. She could tell by his face that something was wrong. When he told her what had happened, she said, "Go back inside and check again. The other piece is going to be there." It was. Susanna's faith made it happen.

The recording session was ending. It was time to make the final payment to László. By now, I had figured out that I could actually cash a check in Hungary, using my American Express card. I made out a check to cash for $10,000, cashed it at a bank, put the money in a bag, and took it quickly to László's office. I didn't want to carry that cash around any longer than I had to! I have to admit that I didn't have $10,000 in my checking account, but I figured it would take a week or two for the check to clear. I was counting on there being some additional money waiting for me when I got home.

On the last day, we had some spare time and for the first time since arriving in Hungary, we relaxed a little. We toured the city, and then, at László's invitation, we had dinner at his home outside of Budapest with all of the recording team and the studio owners. It was a magnificent Hungarian feast; a fitting way to end an experience none of us would ever forget.

Our trip home was complicated by a snarl of delayed flights and missed connections. The airline employees were patient and helpful. They managed to get us on a flight out of Frankfurt to New York. We would have to fly to New York on American Airlines, claim our luggage at Kennedy airport, and then take a cab to La Guardia airport to catch our final flight home on another airline. It would be a difficult transition, but we were eager to get home, any way we could.

When we arrived at Kennedy airport in New York, we found our baggage claim area and waited for our luggage. And waited some more. Finally, it was all too apparent that five of our bags were missing. Evidently, the delayed flights and missed connections had affected the bags too. Unfortunately, the cases that were missing were the most important ones. They contained *Tascam DA 88s*—expensive new digital recording machines—which we had purchased just for this project. Not only were they worth far more than any airline compensation we would receive, should they be lost, but they were also scheduled to be used three days later for the next phase of the recording project, when Paul would record the choral parts in Dallas.

Emily and I had no choice but to leave for La Guardia airport to catch the next leg of our flight. We arranged for the lost bags, if and when they were found, to be sent directly to Paul in Dallas. Saying goodbye to Paul and Stephen, we caught a cab across town to La Guardia and more bad news. Somehow, "the system" had lost our reservation for the flight home, but again, with the help of a kind counter agent, we were able to fly standby, and finally arrived home late Thursday night, exhausted.

I unpacked my garment bag, repacked it with some clean clothes, threw some tapes and CDs in my travel case, and fell into bed for a few hours sleep. Next morning, I flew to Los Angeles.

Paul called from Dallas. The cases with their precious digital recording machines were still missing. We had two options. We could call American Airlines, and we could pray. We did both, long and frequently. Paul called American so often that they begged him not to call anymore. "We don't have any more room to write on this form!" the harried agent told him.

"Well," said Paul logically, "if you don't want us to call, just find our bags."

I called too. And prayed. Friday evening Paul called again. "Jaime, good news!" he yelled into the phone. "American Airlines delivered two bags today!"

"Wonderful! Praise the Lord," I responded. "Now we need three more!"

After Saturday night's concert, Paul called again. "Good news again, Jaime! Two more bags arrived today!"

"Hallelujah! Praise the Lord," I shouted. "Now we need one more!"

Sunday morning came. I had a mini-concert in a church in Yucaipa, and another in Highland, about thirty minutes away. In Dallas, they were setting up for the recording session with the choir. Paul called again. "They found it!" he yelled joyously. "American Airlines just called. They say the last bag is in Salt Lake City—but not to worry—they'll get it on a plane right away, and send it wherever we need it to be." The case arrived at the Dallas-Fort Worth airport, and a courier took it directly to the studio. Paul plugged it in, tested it, and it was fine. The recording session began exactly on time—yet another miracle—another sign that the Lord was with us, another boost for our faith.

Our faith needed all the help it could get. Emily and I were trusting in the Lord completely, but that didn't mean our financial worries went away. We had written checks for money we didn't have and maxed out our credit cards to pay the bills for the project. Then some money would come in, as people ordered the album that wasn't even finished yet. It was just amazing the way the money came when we needed it. Still, there were times when the worry and strain wore us down. Our friends rallied around us. I particularly remember when my friend Salim Burgos and his brother Luis helped us. Salim quietly slipped some money in my pocket—a significant amount. Not long afterwards, Salim asked me how things were going, and when I shared some of our struggles with him, he made another donation—for the exact amount I needed to cover a check I had written.

Emily and I were under severe stress. The sheer amount of effort and traveling necessary to raise money for and promote the new album was taking its toll on our health. We couldn't sleep, even though we were exhausted most of the time. The financial strain was especially great. It was a time of testing for both of us.

Sometime in August 1999, I got a call from Dr. Stephen W. Plate. We had met a couple of years earlier when I played for a YMCA prayer breakfast right there in our hometown of Shelby. He was the conductor of the Charlotte Repertory Orchestra, a fine youth training orchestra, and had suggested that I might solo with this orchestra some day. He was also a faculty member of a Christian university called Gardner-Webb University, in nearby Boiling Springs, North Carolina.

"Jaime," he said, on that day in August. "The university wants to expand its music program. We have a part-time opening on our staff that we'd like to discuss with you."

They were looking for someone to teach violin lessons, play in the faculty string trio, and be the concertmaster of the university orchestra. I agreed to meet with him and the chairman of the music department, and when I did, they offered me the job.

What a wonderful opportunity the Lord had provided for me, just when things were looking so bleak! The university and Dr. Plate were accommodating and helpful—and allowed me to work around my concert schedule.

Teaching violin lessons again brought back a lot of memories. I hadn't taught violin lessons since I was in the 8th grade myself. I had always loved teaching. I had some wonderful students, from very young ones all the way to mature ones, and I enjoyed the opportunity to teach them.

The month of December was shaping up to be the busiest of my life. I sought as many opportunities as possible to promote the Christmas album. I had scheduled twenty-four concerts for the first twenty-one days of the month. Sometimes I'd play at one place in the morning, catch a flight, and play at another place that night. It all worked as long as there were no delayed flights, no hitches. I remember one time that month, when I was supposed to put on a concert sponsored by Sonora Community Hospital, in Sonora, about 150 miles from San Francisco. My flight was delayed, and I was already way behind schedule when I finally arrived in San Francisco and rented

A wonderful holiday family gathering!

Emily's older brother David, his wife Vicki, and their two wonderful children Sarah and Eddie.

Emily's sister, Ashley, her husband, Ronnie, and their two precious kids—Nathan and Nicholas.

a car. They gave me a Mustang, a sports car I don't usually rent—but it would do in a pinch. I took it. I knew I barely had enough time to get to Sonora.

Well, to make a long story short, I got lost. Very lost. My friend Steve Peterson had given me the directions, and I called him on my cell phone. Turns out, I was going in the wrong direction on Interstate 5. If you've ever been on that stretch of road, you know there is nothing there—no exits, no place to turn around—nothing. While Steve was trying to figure out where the nearest exit was, I made an illegal U-turn, skidding across a half a block of dirt, hit the freeway again, stepped on the accelerator, and put that little car to the test. I managed to arrive at the church no more than five or ten minutes late.

On this occasion, Emily had gone ahead of me and was already in Sonora. As I walked into the church, she was doing something I had never seen her do before and I have never seen her do it since. Shy, reserved Emily had gone up on the stage and started a sing-along, while the poor pastor paced back and forth in the foyer. Amazingly enough, that was one of the best concerts of that Christmas season. I thanked the Lord that He had gotten me there safely.

Though I had not pursued personal donations, some of our friends helped out anyway. Don and Alice Merrill, whom I'd known since 1991, gave us a generous gift. Don had "run sound" for me in 1991 in Lodi, California, and I had appointed him my exclusive sound engineer. Dr. Willard and Mrs. Eva Bridwell, from Hanford, California, whom Emily and I had met in Hawaii in 1997, also helped us out financially. Our good friend Ilsa Nation helped in another way. She spent an entire weekend listening to the songs to help us determine the correct order for the album. When we were having our greatest difficulty with the project, she prayed for us every hour on the hour! How can I ever thank these wonderful friends and the countless others who have supported us in so many ways!

There are many more stories of that incredible month that I could tell you, but I think you get the idea. It was filled with miracles. The biggest miracle of all came in January, when we added up the figures on the album project. I had spent $100,000. When we totaled up the income from all the December concerts and album sales, we had just over $101,000. Praise the Lord! All through those difficult days, when it seemed that we were about to go under, the Lord was with us. He provided enough to keep us going, and he had provided what we needed to pay for the album. Once again, I was filled with gratitude for my heavenly Father. He had always led me, and I knew He always would.

Emily and I had planned a vacation for January, knowing we would need it. My booking agent, Linda, and her husband were moving to Australia. They had invited us to spend a skiing week with them in Vail, Colorado before they left.

We enjoyed that wonderful week in the snow and it helped us unwind. It was followed by a week in Hawaii, which we managed to arrange for very little money, using my frequent flyer miles. We rested and relaxed, but even after two weeks of rest, we still felt exhausted. It took us both several months to fully recover from the highs and lows of that Christmas album experience.

As the weeks went by, I began to realize just how impossible the whole project ought to have been. It should have been a dismal failure. It would not have succeeded without the blessing, the guidance and direction, of the Lord. Sometimes I've wondered if my faith is so blind that it borders on stupidity. I still don't know the answer to that question. Did I take chances I should not have taken— did I stretch myself beyond my capacity—to make this project happen? I don't know. Maybe God saw that my motives were right, and saved me from falling into a huge hole. He had done it before. I know He will do it again.

Faith is kind of like a muscle. It needs exercise. If we just do the easy things, God cannot show us His power. I believe God wants us to trust Him completely. So I'm committed to doing big things for the Lord. I want to continue to exercise my faith. I can't say that I want to go through another project like the Christmas album again any time soon, but whether it's an album or something else, I know the Lord will show me the way. By His grace, I want to be ready for that next big challenge, whatever it is. In fact, I'm looking forward to it.

By this time, Emily and I had been married for three years. She had been traveling with me almost constantly. It was tough on her. It's tough on me, but I've been doing it for many years. It seems to me that I'm always jet-lagged, always tired, never really sure whether it's time to eat or sleep. But I'm used to it. Emily, however, jumped into it with both feet all at once when she married me, without any conditioning, and her health suffered as a result. As I've said, she has suffered from severe asthma all her life. When she was a baby, her parents often had to rush her to the emergency room, not knowing if she'd live or die.

Emily's asthma is allergy-based. She is allergic to animals. When we travel, we sometimes stay in people's homes. It has been a particular challenge to try to avoid staying with people who have pets. People say to us, "Oh, we'd love to have you stay with us."

"Thanks," I'd say. Then I'd ask, "Do you guys have pets?" And I'd explain about Emily's asthma.

"Oh, we have a dog," they'd say, or "We have a cat—but it never comes inside the house. You'll be fine." Then we would arrive at the house and discover that just that day the cat or dog had taken a sudden notion to come indoors for a few minutes. People don't understand that having a cat or a dog in the house even once is enough to set Emily on an allergic reaction. She'd have a huge asthma attack, and after suffering through it with her, I'd say, "Never again!"

They say you don't know what you have till it's gone—and we sure take a simple thing like breathing for granted. The first time I saw Emily unable to breathe, I vowed to make sure I never put her in a situation like that again. But it did happen again, no matter how careful we were.

Emily was worn out, tired, completely exhausted, suffering from insomnia as well as asthma. Her immune system was weakened and she needed to take more than her usual medication. Still the asthma attacks came more frequently. We agreed that she should take a sabbatical from travel and stay home until she was well again. I hated leaving her alone so much.

Emily's parents had moved to the Chattanooga, Tennessee area. Her sister, Ashley, who had been married the same year we had, lived with her dentist husband, Ronnie, in Blue Ridge, Georgia. After talking it over, we decided that the best thing for us to do would be to move to Tennessee, so Emily could be closer to her family and friends.

Emily's note: Our lifestyle has taught me to be more patient, more spontaneous, and yes, more independent. When something drastic happens at home while Jaime is traveling, I can't call him to run home and take care of it. Many things tend to happen when he's gone, for some reason. I've dealt with numerous crises: a flooded house, a drunk man who parked himself on my doorstep, having to rush myself to the hospital with bronchitis, and car accidents, just to name a few.

Sometimes people ask me how we stay happily married when we have to be apart so much. I tell them that when we're together, we're really together. We make time to be with each other. When we're apart, we talk on the phone often—usually five times a day or more. Jaime sends me flowers, and I give him cards and do extra little things for him when we're together. When he comes home from a trip, I try to make the house especially welcoming, with candles and soft music. We are probably forced to communicate more than couples who spend all their spare time together—since we can't see nonverbal communication over the phone—so we have to really talk—ask each other questions.

I never expected to leave beautiful North Carolina, but as long as I had an airport nearby, I could manage anywhere. My commitment to Gardner-Webb University complicated things—since my fifteen-minute commute was about to turn into a four-hour drive. I resolved that problem by sometimes staying with my parents on Monday nights, then heading back home on Tuesday after my work at the university. This had the advantage of allowing me to spend more time with Mima and Pipo, and turned out to be a real blessing. On other occasions, I'd stay at the home of Dr. Bobby Jones. His daughter, Bonnie, was one of my students and they graciously welcomed me into their home.

The following year was filled with travel and concertizing. During the last month of the year, I was particularly busy, as I had been the year before. I'll never forget the second weekend of December. On the 9th of that month, I flew to Chicago to perform at a hospital Christmas party for my friend Roger Cary. On Sunday morning, I flew back to Charlotte to present a worship concert at the church where Dr. Stephen Plate was minister of music. My flight was delayed, and, not for the first time, I walked onto the platform as I was being introduced. Fortunately, my good friend Dr. Bill Claytor, with whom I played in the Gardner-Webb University Orchestra, was used to this scenario, and was all ready to run the sound for me. But that was not the end of my weekend! That night, December 10th, I took part in the wedding of my baby sister, May. Emily and I were very happy for May, whose groom, Keith Pohl, is a wonderful Christian young man. What a pleasure it was for me to relax and share in May's happiness!

CHAPTER FIFTEEN

Returning to Cuba

For years, I had been trying to get a visa to go to Cuba. I longed to return to the land of my birth. I was ten years old when I left, so I had many memories of my life there. I have talked with many Cubans who say they never want to go back. Others, like me, long to do so. Pipo had returned once or twice, but I had never been able to manage it. Every time I sought permission, the government would either deny it outright, or grant me approval and then cancel it at the last minute.

Now a new possibility had arisen. I received an invitation to participate in a project to bring the gospel to the people of Cuba through a Spanish-language radio program called La Voz de la Esperanza. This program actually started in Cuba in 1942, but for many years has been based in the United States.

Pastor Frank González, himself a Cuban immigrant, had recently become the new speaker/director for the broadcast. He had had a desire to do something for the people of Cuba for many years. He asked the Cuban government to allow La Voz to conduct a large series of evangelistic meetings in Havana. Many thought such permission would be impossible to get, but the Lord had opened the door, and plans were under way to hold these meetings. Pastor González had kindly invited me to go. Knowing that my request for a visa had been denied several times, he asked someone who was working with the broadcast to handle getting me a visa, along with the rest of the people who were going to participate in the meetings.

If you're an American, it is fairly easy to get a visa to go to Cuba. If you were born there, however, it's much harder. The government insists that you fill out forms with an incredible amount of information. The government already knows most of this information, but they make you come up with it anyway. I had to research all the addresses where my parents had lived in Cuba, the names of relatives living in Cuba, and other bits of information. It was challenging, but not impossible.

Eliseo Lozano was the person responsible for getting visas for the La Voz group. When he went to the office of Cuban Interest and Affairs in Washington, D. C. and asked for my visa, they told him, "We know who Jaime Jorge is. We are going to allow him to go to Cuba on condition that he performs for the National Assembly of Cuba. There is also the possibility that he may be required to perform for Fidel Castro."

When Eliseo reported this conversation to me, I didn't know what to think. Here I was an exiled Cuban, who had fled Cuba with my family twenty years before. Now I was going to have an opportunity to go back to that country, and maybe even play for the very person who has caused my countrymen so much pain and suffering for decades. At first, I felt only rebellion and turmoil. Surely I couldn't do this. However, after praying about it, I had peace with it. I realized that I was not going to Cuba to represent democracy. I was not going to represent my family or my fellow exiled Cubans, or the people who had suffered at the hands of Castro's government. I was going to Cuba to represent the King of kings and Lord of lords. I vowed that, if I should have the opportunity to play for Fidel Castro, with the Lord's help I would behave in a way that would be worthy of a representative of Christ.

As much as I wanted to go to Cuba myself, I wasn't sure I wanted Emily to go with me. She was very interested in going, however. We talked it over, and she persuaded me that it would be a wonderful opportunity for her to see my country and its people, and to learn to know and understand me better as a result.

We began our preparations. Repeatedly, when friends who knew Cuba learned that Emily planned to go, they advised me, "Make sure she never has to go to a hospital." As much as Castro and his propagandists would like the world to believe that there is great medical care in Cuba, the truth is far different. Medical supplies and equipment are scarce, and the health and hygiene practiced in hospitals puts visitors (or anyone) at risk. So we made sure that Emily had all her medications. If an asthma attack happened in Cuba, she would have what she needed.

The Cuban government, many months previously, had agreed upon the dates for this evangelistic trip, and detailed plans were under way. Just a few weeks before the meetings were to start, the government changed the dates. There was a wild scramble to change plane tickets and arrangements, providing a challenge for the planners of the trip.

Meanwhile, I had learned that La Voz de la Esperanza wanted to take Bibles to Cuba. I had heard that there was a waiting list for every Bible in Cuba. I began raising money at my concerts to help buy Bibles for the Cuban people.

As the date of the trip drew closer, I grew both excited and fearful. I had my Cuban passport and we had our visas, ready to go. I was thankful that Emily was going with me, eager to share this experience with her. My good friend Steve Peterson was also going to accompany us. I was grateful that he had managed to take some time from his busy medical practice. Steve's presence has always been a source of encouragement for me.

We Cubans who were going on this trip felt real fear. Some might think it isn't realistic, but that fear is in the back of the mind of every Cuban returning to his homeland. We had been warned that we could expect to be shadowed by Cuban secret service agents every moment we were in the country. We knew that our rooms would be bugged. It was an uneasy feeling.

"What happens if they don't let you out of Cuba?" Emily had asked me only half-jokingly when we discussed the trip some months before. "What if they keep you there?"

"Well," I replied, "You come back without me."

"I don't think so," my wife responded. "I'm going to stay with you!"

"Emily," I said, "If for some reason they didn't allow me to leave, the best thing you could do for me would be to come back to the United States and get yourself on every television show you possibly could to try to drum up support for getting me back."

We tried to be lighthearted about it, but there was an uneasiness, a sense of apprehension, all the same.

At last the time came, and our Aero Caribe flight arrived at José Martí Airport outside Havana on February 13, 2000, and our group went through the lengthy customs procedures. Finally we were outside the terminal. I looked around, and took a deep breath. I found it hard to believe that I was breathing Cuban air for the first time in over twenty years.

Our meetings were held in one of the largest theaters in Havana, just across the street from the Cuban equivalent of the FBI. Almost 2,000 people attended every night, including, we were told, dozens of plain-clothes secret agents. The La Voz team presented the gospel in an exciting and powerful way. The programs were being videotaped for broadcast to other Spanish-speaking countries.

As I stood up to play on the first night, my heart was beating fast. I knew, from messages I had received that there were old friends of my family in the audience—people that I hadn't seen in twenty years. I wanted to make a good impression for Mima and Pipo's sake. I also wanted to represent my adopted country well, but most of all, I wanted to witness for my Lord. I was under tremendous pressure. As I played, it seemed to me that I was messing up royally, but when I looked at the video later, I realized with relief that I hadn't played too badly.

After the first few days of meetings, we had a free weekend. I was looking forward to traveling to the city of Santa Clara, in the central part of the island, to visit my family, including my grandfather and his wife, aunts and uncles. Pipo was coming to Cuba on Friday especially to see his father, my grandfather or *abuelo,* who at ninety-three was in failing health. The plan was for him to be driven to Santa Clara, and then Emily and I would meet him there on Sunday.

Early Sunday morning, Luis Alberto Gómez came to pick us up in his 1951 turquoise Chevy for the trip to Santa Clara. I had known Luis Alberto and his brother, Luis Arturo, when we were kids. Luis Arturo and I were actually closer in age, and had been good friends. Tragically, Luis Arturo was killed in an accident several years before my visit to Cuba. Luis Alberto and I embraced each other for the first time in twenty years. It was an emotional moment.

Emily, Steve Peterson and I piled into Luis Alberto's elderly car for the drive to Santa Clara. The distance was not particularly great, but the condition of the road—not to mention my eager anticipation—made the trip seem long. As we drove, we reviewed my mental list of places to see and people to meet. The list wasn't very long— but we wanted to make sure we didn't miss any of the important places or people.

As we drove into town, I began to recognize some familiar places. To my eyes, everything seemed old, shabby, and small. It felt like a scene from an old movie, or like being stuck in a time warp. Our first stop was to be my grandfather's house. As we drove toward his neighborhood, I suddenly had a strange familiar feeling. "Luis Alberto," I asked, "is there any chance that my old violin teacher, Adolfo Guimbarda, used to live around here?"

"Yes, indeed," Luis Alberto replied, "very near here." Eagerly I asked Luis Alberto if we could stop there on our way to my grandfather's house. I knew that both Mr. Guimbarda and his wife had died shortly before, but I was hoping to see some of his family members. I had stayed in touch with Mr. Guimbarda through the years. He was a gifted violinist and a great teacher. I was deeply indebted to him for my early training. I had occasionally sent him small gifts from the United States, and had had a great desire to see him again. It was one of the reasons I had been seeking a Cuban visa for several years.

Luis Alberto had also taken lessons from Mr. Guimbarda for a short time, so he knew exactly where his house was, and he soon parked the Chevy outside it. I walked up to the door and knocked, and when no one came, I looked in the window. His daughter, María, was standing there, and as soon as she saw me, her hands flew to her face, and she said, "Oh my God! I don't believe it! It's Jaime!"

She flung the door open and I walked into the living room of the house where I had taken lessons for five years. Everything was the same; even the furniture hadn't changed in twenty years. Emily and Steve were right behind me—Emily with a video camera and Steve snapping one still shot after another. I was transported back to 1975, and remembered how Mr. Guimbarda, the concertmaster of the Santa Clara City Orchestra, had lovingly, carefully, and patiently taught a little five-year-old boy how to play the violin. I still use the basic techniques I learned in that small living room. I also remembered some of the things I had said to upset him—how angry I was when he told my mother that I had to practice every single day. How I regretted those outbursts!

I had a wonderful time talking with Mr. Guimbarda's daughter, María. Her brother Adolfo, Jr., had been a close friend of Pipo's, and she had lots of stories to tell about their times together. At one point she opened a drawer and showed me the things I had sent to her father over the years—letters, pens, and other little gifts. He had kept them all.

I translated as much as I could for Emily and Steve, but I found myself so choked with emotion that it was difficult not to cry. I held back the tears as best I could. Crying didn't seem appropriate. After all, I was the one who had been able to leave Cuba's oppression and poverty behind. Those emotions surfaced repeatedly as we visited with other friends and family members.

Next, we headed for my grandfather's house. It had been fourteen years since I had seen Abuelo and his wife, Nena. Our biological grandmother had died of a heart attack before May and I were born, so Nena has always been our grandmother. We had a little trouble finding the right house. All I could recall was that it was near the baseball stadium. After a few wrong turns, we found what

Hugging Abuelo when we first saw each other. He wears the glove because of arthritis in his hand (no similarity to Michael Jackson).

My concert at Abuelo's house (Alberto, Pipo, Abuelo, Nena)

I thought was the right street corner—but there was a police station there. We gave up and called Abuelo. In a couple of minutes, Pipo showed up, riding a bike—the most reliable mode of transportation in Cuba—and escorted us back to Abuelo's house.

As soon as Abuelo saw me, he began to call out my name, "Jaime, Jaime, Jaime!" He threw his skinny arms around me and wouldn't let go. "I'm going to bite your ear—how do you like that?" he asked. Emily and Steve laughed. I'd told them about Abuelo's ear-nibbling habit.

As I looked at this old man who was so dear to me, I thought, *He can bite my ear all he wants—I'm not going to mind.* We held onto each other, talking and laughing. Then he spied Emily. "My granddaughter Emíl!" he cried. In my phone conversations with Abuelo, I had been talking about Emily ever since the two of us began dating back in 1995. Abuelo's hearing isn't good, and combined with his difficulty with the English language, he's never managed to get Emily's name right. To him, she's always "Emíl."

We sat down to lunch at the very same table where May and I had often eaten as children. As I looked across the table at Nena, memories came flooding back, of how she had fed us special treats and told us stories of Peter Pan, Snow White and the Seven Dwarfs. Now, all these years later, what a wonderful time we had! Pipo, Abuelo, Nena, Emily, my childhood friend Luis Alberto, and my good friend Steve, all together, all laughing and talking at the same time! Then Pipo gave us a tour of the house. Even though it was shabby and simply furnished, it was spacious and comfortable by Cuban standards. All through the house there were pictures of our family, including my posters and album covers—something that touched me deeply.

Later we drove through the grounds of the former El Colegio de Las Antillas, close to my old neighborhood. Everything looked shabby and abandoned. The trees, once tall and stately markers on either side of the original entryway, were mostly gone. The once beautiful buildings were falling down, their paint was peeling.

Suddenly, Luis Alberto stopped the Chevy. "Here we are!" he announced. I looked around in surprise and dismay. This couldn't be my old neighborhood! Everything was so small, so changed. But there it was, the house I'd grown up in. A second story had been added since we lived there. Luis Alberto told me that the people who now lived in the house were faithful Christians, and would probably be happy to have me visit. Luis Alberto's childhood home was just across a narrow walkway. He walked over to take a look at his old house, and I went to see mine.

I knocked on the door and waited. A young woman came to the door, a sleeping baby in her arms. "Good afternoon, sister," I said. I told her my name and explained that I had once lived in her house. "Do you think we could come in and take a look around?" I asked, gesturing behind me at Emily and Steve.

"Of course!" she replied, stepping aside. She must have wondered if we were investigating her as Emily began filming with her camcorder and Steve snapped pictures with his camera. I looked around me. I was dumbfounded. Even with the additions and expansions, this was a matchbox of a house. I walked from room to room, showing Emily and Steve where my parents' bed had been, where first my crib was, and where later the bunk beds May and I slept in had been. I showed them where the piano had stood in the living room, and where my dad had had his study. As I tried to describe Pipo's big desk to them, my voice broke. The memories were too much for me.

As we prepared to leave, I thanked the lady for allowing us to see the house. I pulled some money out of my pocket to give her a thank-you gift. I had saved up for months before coming to Cuba in order to have some money to give away. There was so much absolute need here that I wanted to give a little something to as many people as I possibly could. Steve, too, had brought a significant amount of money, in ones, fives, and tens, for the same purpose. But the lady refused to take our money. "I'd much rather that you pray for us," she said.

"Would you like us to pray right here and now?" I asked. She agreed, and we all bowed our heads and prayed together. I assured her that we would never forget her and would continue to remember her daily in our prayers.

Our house in Santa Clara (Colegio de Las Antillas). The second floor and an addition at the back had been added since we lived there.

Emily, me, Pipo, Abuelo, Nena, Ester Lilia (Nena's daughter), and Steve on my last visit with Abuelo.

The Machados had lived right next door to us—and had left Cuba with us in 1980. There was a lady named Irone who had lived with them. I had always wondered what had become of her. To my great surprise and joy, she was still there! We visited briefly with her and with other families on the street. Even former communist families came out and greeted us—I call them former communists because the only real communists in Cuba are the ones in power—the others pay lip service to communism, but they hate it.

I remembered all my favorite places—where we had had our snail races, where we had played hide and seek, and all the other games that boys play. Emily had been quiet during the visit to my old house. As we left, she said something to me I'll never forget. "I've always told you that you are a dreamer, Jaime, but now that I've seen what and where you came from, I can understand why."

I know I'm a dreamer. I'm constantly telling Emily "we're going to do this one of these days," or "we're going to do that, or go there." Her words reminded me of one of my favorite songs, "The Impossible Dream." By allowing me to return to Cuba, God had given me the chance to live my impossible dream. As we left that little Cuban house where my life on this earth began, I thanked the Lord again for all He had given me—for His forgiveness, for His grace, and for the opportunity I have to share His love with others.

By now it was getting late in the day, but I had one more place to go. I was giving a concert that night in the little church in Santa Clara where I began my performing career. In fact, to accommodate the crowds, there would be two concerts, back to back, one for out-of-town guests who were coming by bus, and then one for the local residents.

That night I played "How Great Thou Art," and Steve played with me on the sax as we played "The Old Rugged Cross." Emily sang "It's My Desire," and finally, I played a song that's one of my greatest favorites: "The Holy City." In Cuba, people don't clap in church. They say, "Amen" instead. That night, the "Amens" were loud and powerful. After "The Holy City," the "Amen" was so thunderous, it seemed to shake the building. What an incredible evening that was. Sometimes, during the performance, Steve and Emily and I would look at each other without a word, and just smile. We knew we were living "The Impossible Dream."

The next day was Monday. In the morning, we stopped by Abuelo's house again. Abuelo and Nena are both very hard of hearing, and talking with them on the phone from the United States was very difficult. The connection is usually poor, anyway, and we had to shout every word for them to understand. Steve had brought the materials with him to make molds of their ears and ear canals, so that we could have hearing aids made for them in the States. We knew that these hearing aids would make a wonderful difference in their ability to hear.

Abuelo didn't want me to go. His tears flowed freely. I struggled to keep my tears inside. Since he and Nena hadn't been able to attend the concert the night before, I gave them a mini-concert before I left. You can be sure I played loud, so they could hear me!

Pipo joined us for our final visit in Santa Clara. The Pentóns were wonderful Christian people and good friends of my parents. Pipo told me that we had often visited in their home when I was a child— but I couldn't remember these occasions. However, when I saw their furniture, their piano, a shelf with its Spanish dolls, the memories flooded back. I recalled that we had wonderful feasts in their home— and they had prepared a bountiful lunch for us and other friends on this Monday afternoon. We ate until we nearly burst.

At the Pentónses' house, I saw some other good friends. Idelkys was the sister of my old friend Roaidis, and Maribel was his mother. Let me tell you the story of Roaidis. We were about the same age, and grew up together in Santa Clara. Roaidis, whom I called Roy, and his family stayed behind in Cuba when we immigrated to the United States. I missed my friend, and we stayed in touch by mail. In 1988, when I was in college at Loyola University, he wrote me a letter with a special request. "Jaime, I'd like to know if you can do one thing for me. I have either grown out of or worn out the clothes I wear to church. Do you think you could send me a suit from

America that I can wear to church?" I remembered that Roy liked to wear his best for Jesus. He always took pride in looking good when he went to church.

When I read these words, I thought about all the suits in my closet. I had so much and he had so little! Rather than send him one of my old suits, I resolved to purchase a brand new suit, with a shirt, tie, shoes, and socks. I wanted Roy to look good for Jesus.

I put the letter in my pile of things to do—and unfortunately, in the busy press of college life, forgot about it. Days, weeks, and months passed. One day, when I came home from school, I found Mima looking very sad. "What's the matter?" I asked.

"I got a phone call from Cuba this morning," she replied. "Roaidis's mother called to tell us that her son had just been killed in an auto accident."

Immediately I remembered his letter to me, and his request. I turned and ran to my bedroom, and searched frantically until I found his letter. "Jaime, I'd like to know if you can do one thing for me," I read, through tear-filled eyes. *If only I could have remembered to send him a new suit, so that he would have had something nice to wear to church before he died!* I agonized. I felt so bad about neglecting this dear friend's request.

Now, years later, after our meal at the Pentón family's house, Roaidis's mother brought out her son's violin. She told me that Roy had started taking violin lessons after I left Santa Clara. For years, he had told his mother that he was looking forward to playing a duet with me someday. The sadness, remorse, and guilt flooded over me again, as they have so many times.

Then she told me something else. I had never learned how Roaidis had died. His mother said that he was working at several different jobs at the time, trying to make a decent living. One night, instead of coming home from his day job, he called her to say that he was going to Havana to work instead. Then, she told me, Roaidis had said something unexpected. "Mom, you know I love you very much. I have drifted from the Lord before, but I want you to know that I have come back. I have a feeling that something is going to happen to me soon. But I want you to know that if something does, I've given my heart to Jesus, and I'm ready to meet Him."

That night, Roaidis climbed onto a truck to get a ride to Havana. Evidently, he was on top of the truck, literally sitting on the roof. Apparently, the driver fell asleep at the wheel, losing control of the truck for a second, and running into a ditch. As he jerked the steering wheel back towards the road, the sudden change in direction sent Roaidis flying off the top of the truck. He hit his head on a rock, and was killed instantly.

As Maribel and Idelkys shared this story with me, their eyes were dry. I fought hard for composure as I translated their words for Steve and Emily. However, Roaidis's mother and sister were so comforted by the knowledge that their son and brother had given his heart to the Lord that they were actually smiling. What a blessed hope we have! I long for the day when I'll be able to see Roaidis again in heaven.

By this time, it was getting late, so after a marathon of photograph taking and a beautiful circle of prayer, Emily, Steve, and I climbed back into Luis Alberto's funky turquoise Chevy and headed back to Havana. It was very quiet in the car on the way to Havana. Each of us was occupied with our own thoughts. Our hearts were full with the experiences of the day.

The Lord was blessing the evangelistic meetings mightily. All over Cuba, dozens of satellite evangelistic efforts were taking place. People from all over the United States had responded to La Voz De La Esperanza's call to preach the gospel in Cuba. They were doing an incredible job, and God was working miracles.

In Havana, nearly two thousand people filled the theater every night to hear the gospel preached. Every night for nine nights, a different group came. These meetings were the fruition of another "Impossible Dream," this time the dream of Frank González, the speaker/director of La Voz, who was born in Cuba. His father was not a religious man, but had fought to overthrow Castro's dictatorship. The government arrested him and he was imprisoned for many years. Even though he was in prison, he managed, after years of maneuvering, to get his wife and son out of Cuba. Frank, Sr.'s last words to his son were, "You're going to a country where God is God; a country that is truly the land of the free and the home of the brave. Be brave! Be free!"

Frank González has dedicated himself to preaching the gospel, and he has had a great burden for the people of Cuba all his life. Frank is a man of God. Knowing him has been a great privilege and blessing to me. His dream was a powerful one. It took a long time for him to work through all the problems, but after a succession of miraculous interventions, the Cuban government gave their permission for a series of meetings in Cuba—the first to be held there in forty-two years.

I had been involved with the preparations for this project since October of 2000. Infected with Frank's passion and fire, I solicited funds for the Cuba project in all the places I visited—raising money especially to buy Bibles.

Finally, the event was taking place. There were countless challenges, obstacles, and problems—but the Lord protected, and nothing ever interrupted the meetings; not a power failure or any other problems.

On the final Tuesday night, I was asked to close the entire event by playing Handel's "Hallelujah Chorus"—my favorite music of all time. "King of kings! Lord of lords" the beautiful tones rang out in that Cuban theater—and for a moment we were all one, no differences, no inequalities. It was a taste of heaven.

All during my visit to Cuba, I had fought back my tears, holding inside as best I could all the joy, sadness, anger, and fear. But not that night. After I finished playing, while Frank led the audience in a closing prayer, I slipped backstage, found a dark, empty room, and began to weep. "Thank You, Jesus, for allowing me to live in the United States of America—and thank You for allowing me to visit my homeland again after all these years. Come soon, Jesus, and take us all home." I prayed, too, for my ten million Cuban brothers and sisters who had suffered through the unspeakable misery of the Castro regime for more than forty-two years.

CHAPTER SIXTEEN

Going Home

How can I explain how I, as a Cuban-American, feel about communism? I love Cuba. I don't hate Castro, although many Cubans do. There is a fire that burns within us—a hatred for communism and what it has done to our country. I hate it because it doesn't work. My family and I have seen its results first-hand. Fidel Castro and the Cuban government have committed many injustices and atrocities in its name. My own family has suffered, but many others suffered much more. You remember the Bay of Pigs affair. It was an unsuccessful invasion of Cuba on April 17, 1961, at Bahía de Cochinos (the Bay of Pigs) by less than two thousand Cubans who had gone into exile in America after the 1959 revolution. Encouraged by members of the United States's Central Intelligence Agency, who trained them, the invaders believed they would have air and naval support from the United States and that the invasion would cause the people of Cuba to rise up and overthrow the regime of Fidel Castro. Neither expectation materialized.

Nevertheless, the Cuban exiles fought with incredible bravado and zeal. However, Cuban army troops pinned them down and forced them to surrender within seventy-two hours. Hundreds were killed, and hundreds more were imprisoned under horrible and inhumane conditions. These and other political and religious prisoners were forced to work eighteen hours a day, and were fed rotten food. A man I know who survived this imprisonment told me that often, the soldiers would sound an alarm during the night, and force the naked inmates to march single file between columns of soldiers. These soldiers had bats, billy clubs, and bayonets. As the prisoners ran through this gauntlet, they were badly beaten. They would be kept outside while soldiers searched their quarters, and then allowed back in.

On one occasion, the soldiers found a little New Testament belonging to a Christian prisoner and confiscated it. When the man returned to his cell and found that his Bible was gone, he asked to speak with the person in charge. "I am going on a hunger strike until you return my New Testament," he quietly informed the soldier.

"Throw him in solitary confinement until he gives up," the soldier ordered. For forty-seven days, this faithful Christian maintained his hunger strike. He finally died, and his body was left to rot where it lay in the solitary confinement cell.

When the prisoners realized that the Christian had been allowed to die, they revolted. The man who told me this story was a leader of this revolt. The soldiers fired machine guns at the prisoners, and he was wounded. A bullet destroyed one of his testicles. When the soldiers found him, they dragged him, bleeding and badly hurt, into the same solitary confinement cell where the body of the Christian lay. This brave man took a spoon and rubbed it against the iron bars of his cell. When the spoon became red-hot, he placed it on the wound in order to cauterize it and protect himself against infection. Today this man is part of an organization in the United States that fights against the Castro regime. There are hundreds of stories like these that every Cuban exile knows. They fill our minds and hearts. We love our beautiful country and its warm-hearted people, but we hate communism, and grieve for the sadness and pain it has caused.

Here's another example of communism's evil effects. The morning after the final evangelistic meeting, we made a two-hour drive from Havana to visit Varadero Beach, one of the longest white sand beaches in the world, and certainly one of the most beautiful. I remembered Mima and Pipo bringing me here when I was sick with rheumatic fever, and I had fond memories of this lovely place. Now it had become an exclusive tourist mecca—a place where Cubans were not allowed to go. Our driver and another Cuban friend were allowed through security as our "tour guides." We found a stretch of beautiful beach and relaxed in lawn chairs, absorbing the sun and the view. Before long, one of the security guards approached our group and told our Cuban friends that they couldn't use the chairs.

A light seemed to go out in the Cuban boy's eyes, as he explained to us that this was a way of life in Cuba. Cubans are second-class citizens in their own country. They cannot stay in a hotel, even if they could afford it. They cannot buy property or a car. He begged us to help get him and his family out—a plea we heard many times during our visit, and continue to hear.

Recently I received a plea from Roaidis's sister Idelkys: "Dear Jaime: I am desperate to leave any way I can. I would like to leave with my husband and son. If you can get me an invitation or a work permit, we will more than repay you all the expenses. If you can't help us, please give us the name of someone who can. I don't have anyone else to go to. Please help me."

There are countless stories like this one. I have made many appeals in my travels for money to help buy Bibles for Cuba, as well to supply clothing, food, soap, toothpaste—items we Americans consider bare necessities. In Cuba, they are incredible luxuries. Many people have helped. Not long ago, an eight-year-old boy sent me four dollars, with this note: "Dear Mr. Jorge: I'm only paying for one Bible because that's all the money I have." A Bible in Cuba costs four dollars.

Incidentally, if you would like to help with any of these projects, please write to La Voz De La Esperanza, Attention: Jaime Jorge, 101 W.

Cochran Street, Simi Valley, California 93065. All such gifts are tax-deductible, of course, and your assistance will be much appreciated.

For Emily and me, it was time to say goodbye to Cuba. Early on a Thursday morning, we arrived at José Martí airport for our journey home. Luis Alberto met us there. We embraced one last time, and said Goodbye. It's my sincere hope and prayer that one of these days before too long, Luis Alberto will be able to leave Cuba. We're working now to help him get his exit visa.

The plane lifted off, and we were on our way back to a different world. I had three concerts to give that weekend, and they felt very different from the ones I had given just two weeks before. I was different. Going to Cuba had changed me. Steve and Emily felt the same way.

I turned thirty in 2000. I have thought long and hard about the fact that Jesus began His ministry at thirty. After returning from Cuba, I felt a tremendous sense of renewal. It seemed to me that the Lord had given me the opportunity to begin my ministry for Him anew—with new gratitude and new insights into His character and His care for me. Once again, I was deeply impressed that God had a plan for my life. I was more grateful than ever before that He had given me the opportunity to grow up and live and serve Him in the United States of America. The visit to my homeland had only reinforced what I already knew—Cuba is not my home! Cuba is where I was born, but America is where I belong. How blessed I feel to live in a country that was founded on the principle of freedom—of both civil and religious liberty.

But America is not my home, either. My home, and yours, too, if you believe in Jesus, is in heaven. What a wonderful privilege we have to use our freedom to tell others about Jesus, and what He has done for us! How I want to be more like Him!

As I look back on my life thus far, I can see that the most difficult, lowest points came when I was furthest from Jesus. How I wasted my time and talent! Satan has so many temptations to hurl at us—especially when we're young. Sometimes it's drugs or alcohol. Sometimes it's pornography, partying, pre-marital sex, or the wrong kind of music. The list goes on and on. If you've read this far, you know I've squandered precious time, energy, and resources chasing some of these very rainbows. But let me share with you something I've learned through it all. The Lord has had His hand over me from my earliest years. Even in my rebellious youth, when I rejected His leading, He never gave up on me. Jesus forgives us. He has plans for us. Jesus wants us to dream big for Him. When we focus on that great truth, it's a lot harder for the devil to tempt us.

At the ripe old age of thirty-something, I have devised an anagram for success, based on dreaming those big dreams. Here it is:

D—Daretaker—be one for God
R—Relationships—guard them carefully
E—Establish goals—then follow through
A—Act on your dream (or Accept God's forgiveness for your mistakes)
M—Motivation—keep your dream God-centered

H—Humility—don't lose sight of the Source of your success
U—Utilize time, energy, and resources carefully
G—God—make Him Number One
E—Enjoy life. God will bless you, so be ready!

My friend, I don't know if you've ever given your life to Jesus. If you haven't, I beg you to do so right now as you read this. Turn your life over to Him. Maybe you don't know how to do it. Just say this prayer: "Jesus, I want to be Your child. I want You to be the Ruler of my life. Forgive me of my sins. Give me a brand new start, and help me love You and obey You. Let the world see You through me. Amen."

If you've already given your heart to Jesus, I urge you, with me, to re-commit your life right now. I want to do so daily. Let's vow together to be instruments of His love. I've asked God to mend the broken strings of my life, and I know He has. He doesn't want my life or yours to be broken. Let's ask God to make us an instrument on which the Master can play beautiful music from now until we are with Him together in heaven.

Emily Jorge—
the love of my
life.

If you have enjoyed reading Jaime's autobiography, you'll be glad to know that his music is available on CD and cassette through Chapel® Music, a division of Pacific Press®. Recent releases include *Christmas in the Aire,* recorded in Europe with the seventy-five-member Hungarian National Orchestra. To order or for more information, call 1-800-765-6955, or go to pacificpress.com/chapel/jorge. Or write to Chapel® Music at 1350 N. Kings Road, Nampa, ID 83653, and ask for a free catalog.

Additional copies of this book may be obtained by calling 1-800-765-6955, or go to abcasap.com.